Richard Conyers

A Collection of Psalms and Hymns, From Various Authors

For the Use of Serious and Devout Christians of Every Denomination

Richard Conyers

A Collection of Psalms and Hymns, From Various Authors
For the Use of Serious and Devout Christians of Every Denomination

ISBN/EAN: 9783744784061

Printed in Europe, USA, Canada, Australia, Japan

Cover: Foto ©Lupo / pixelio.de

More available books at **www.hansebooks.com**

A COLLECTION

OF

PSALMS AND HYMNS,

FROM

VARIOUS AUTHORS:

FOR THE USE OF

SERIOUS AND DEVOUT CHRISTIANS

OF ALL

DENOMINATIONS.

WORSHIP THE LORD IN THE BEAUTY OF HOLINESS.   PSALM xxix. 2.

LONDON,

Printed by T. and J. W. PASHAM, in Black-Friars.

MDCCLXVII.

A COLLECTION

OF

PSALMS AND HYMNS.

HYMN I.

✠ INVITATION.

1 COME, ye sinners, poor and wretched,
　　Weak and wounded, sick and sore,
　Jesus ready stands to save you,
　　Full of pity, love and pow'r,
　　　He is able,
　He is willing, doubt no more.

2 Ho! ye needy, come and welcome,
　　God's free bounty glorify:
　True belief, and true repentance,
　　Ev'ry grace that brings us nigh,
　　　Without money
　Come to Jesus Christ and buy.

3 Let

[4]

3 Let not confcience make you linger,
    Nor of fitnefs fondly dream;
  All the fitnefs he requireth,
    Is to feel your need of him.
      This he gives you,
    'Tis the Spirit's glimm'ring beam.

4 Agonizing in the garden,
    Lo! your maker proftrate lies!
  On the bloody tree behold him,
    Hear him cry before he dies,
      " It is finifh'd."
    Sinner will not this fuffice?

5 Lo! th' incarnate God afcended,
    Pleads the merit of his blood;
  Venture on him, venture freely,
    Let no other truft intrude.
      None but Jefus
    Can do helplefs finners good.

6 Saints and angels join'd in concert,
    Sing the praifes of the lamb,
  While the blifsful feats of heaven
    Sweetly echo with his name.
      Hallelujah!
    Sinners here may do the fame.

HYMN

HYMN II.

✠ ANOTHER.

1 SInners obey the gospel-word,
   Haste to the supper of your Lord,
   Be wise to know your gracious day,
   All things are ready, come away.

2 Ready the Father is to own,
   And kiss his late returning son;
   Ready the loving Saviour stands,
   And spreads for you his bleeding hands.

3 Ready the Spirit of his love,
   Just now the stony heart to move;
   T'apply, and witness with the blood,
   And wash, and seal you, sons of God.

4 Ready for you the angels wait,
   To triumph in your blest estate:
   Tuning their harps, they long to praise
   The wonders of redeeming grace.

5 Come then, ye sinners, to your Lord,
   To happiness in Christ restor'd;
   His proffer'd benefits embrace,
   And taste the fulness of his grace.

HYMN III.

ANOTHER.

1 LET ev'ry mortal ear attend,
    And ev'ry heart rejoice,
The trumpet of the gospel sounds
    With an inviting voice.

2 Come all ye hungry starved souls,
    That feed upon the wind,
And vainly strive, with earthly toys,
    To fill an empty mind.

3 Eternal wisdom has prepar'd
    A soul-reviving feast;
And bids your longing appetites
    The rich provision taste.

4 Ho! ye that pant for living streams,
    And pine away and die;
Here you may quench your raging thirst
    With springs that never dry.

5 Rivers of love and mercy here
    In a rich ocean join;
Salvation in abundance flows,
    Like floods of milk and wine.

6 Dear God! the treasures of thy love
   Are everlasting mines;
   Deep as our boundless miseries are,
   And boundless as our sins.

7 The happy gates of gospel-grace
   Stand open night and day;
   Lord, we are come to seek supplies,
   And drive our wants away.

HYMN IV.

ANOTHER.

1 COME sinners, to the gospel-feast,
   Let ev'ry soul be Jesu's guest;
   Ye need not one be left behind,
   For God hath bidden all mankind.

2 "Have me excus'd," why will ye say,
   From health, and life, and liberty;
   From all that is in Jesus giv'n
   From pardon, holiness, and heav'n!

3 Come then ye souls by sin opprest,
   Ye weary wand'rers after rest;
   Ye poor and maimed, halt and blind,
   In Christ an hearty welcome find.

4 See him set forth before your eyes,
   Behold the bleeding sacrifice!
   His offer'd love let all embrace,
   And freely now be sav'd by grace.

5 Ye who believe his record true,
   Shall sup with him, and he with you;
   Come to the feast, be sav'd from sin,
   For Jesus waits to take you in.

6 This is the time, no more delay,
   This is the glorious gospel-day;
   Come in this moment at his call,
   And live to him, who dy'd for all.

HYMN V.

THE SAME.

1 SInners behold the pierced Lamb,
    For you he hung upon the stem;
   Behold him by the eye of faith,
   For life doth issue from his death.

2 Salvation's well wide open stands,
   And blood-streams run from feet and hands;
   The open'd side doth richly flow,
   From whence, with joy, we water draw.

3 Water

3 Water to quench our parching thirst,
To cleanse and make us fit for Christ;
T'allay our nature's fire within,
And purify the soul from sin.

4 Jesus alone true life imparts,
And med'cine for all wounded hearts;
With balm supplies for ev'ry sore,
And works a speedy, perfect cure.

5 One look to him upon the pole
Revives and heals the sin-stung soul;
Relieves the weary and the faint,
The tempted and each mourner's want.

6 Come then thou great high-priest apply
To us this sov'reign remedy;
That we the blessings of thy death
May antedate below by faith.

HYMN VI.

THE SAME.

1 YE weary wanderers draw near,
    That know no solid peace or rest,
Lay by each doubt and anxious fear,
    And lean upon your Saviour's breast:
All's stolen fruit that can be found
To chear the soul on nature's ground.

2 Come,

2 Come, for the gospel bids you come,
   Jesus for sinners bled and dy'd;
The sacred word reports there's room,
   The Lamb he wooes you for his bride;
Your souls shall find a resting place
In arms of everlasting grace.

3 The day of small things don't despise,
   By poverty encrease your store;
The happy soul, that's truly wise,
   Can richer grow by being poor:
To melt in love, to sink in shame,
This be my wish, be that my flame.

4 Give me a sympathizing soul,
   To bear thy suff'rings on my heart,
Thy pain, and agonizing toil,
   Nor let me from this vision part;
Then shall I heartily rejoice,
And raise to thee my grateful voice.

5 All earthly objects now give way,
   Nature and creature both resign;
On thee by faith myself I'll stay,
   And taste the pow'r of love divine;
Redemption in thy blood is found,
My anchor's cast on sacred ground.

HYMN VII.

AT THE OPENING OF WORSHIP.

1 NOW may the Spirit's holy fire,
    Descending from above,
His waiting family inspire
    With joy, and peace, and love!

2 Thee we the Comforter confess;
    Unless thou'rt present here;
Our songs of praise are vain address,
    We utter heartless pray'r.

3 Wake heav'nly wind, arise, and come,
    Blow on the drooping field;
Our spices then shall breathe perfume,
    And fragrant incense yield.

4 Touch, with a living coal, the lip
    That shall proclaim thy word;
And bid each awful hearer keep
    Attention to the Lord.

5 Hasten the restitution-day,
    Which now corruption shrouds;
New heav'ns, and new earth display,
    With Jesus in the clouds.

HYMN VIII.

ANOTHER.

1 ONCE more we come before our God,
    Once more his blessing ask;
O may not duty seem a load,
    Nor worship prove a task!

2 Father, thy quick'ning Spirit send
    From heav'n in Jesu's name,
To make our waiting minds attend,
    And put our souls in frame.

3 May we receive the word we hear,
    Each in an honest heart;
Hoard up the precious treasure there,
    And never with it part.

4 To seek thee all our hearts dispose,
    To each thy blessing suit;
And let the seed thy servant sows
    Produce a plent'ous fruit.

5 Bid the refreshing north-wind wake;
    Say to the south-wind blow;
Let ev'ry plant the pow'r partake,
    And all the garden grow.

6 Revive

6 Revive the parch'd with heav'nly show'rs,
    The cold with warmth divine;
And as the benefit is ours,
    Be all the glory thine.

HYMN IX.

ANOTHER.

1 COME, ye sinners come to Jesus,
    Think upon your gracious Lord;
   He has pity'd your condition,
He has sent his gospel-word.
     Mercy calls you,
Mercy flows on Jesu's blood.

2   Dearest Saviour help thy servant
To proclaim thy wond'rous love;
   Pour thy grace upon this people,
That thy truth they may approve
     Bless, O bless them
From thy shining courts above.

3   Now thy gracious word invites them
To partake the gospel-feast;
   Let thy Spirit sweetly draw them,
Ev'ry soul be Jesu's guest.
     O receive us,
Let us find thy promis'd rest.

HYMN X.

ANOTHER.

1 LORD, we come before thee now,
   At thy feet we humbly bow:
Oh! do not our suit disdain,
Shall we seek thee, Lord, in vain?

2 Lord, on thee our souls depend,
In compassion now descend:
Fill our hearts with thy rich grace,
Tune our lips to sing thy praise.

3 In thine own appointed way,
Now we seek thee, here we stay;
Lord we know not how to go
'Till a blessing thou bestow.

4 Send some message from thy word,
That may joy and peace afford;
Let thy Spirit now impart
Full salvation to each heart.

5 Comfort those who weep and mourn,
Let the time of joy return;
Those that are cast down, lift up,
Make them strong in faith and hope!

6 Grant that all may seek and find
  Thee a God gracious and kind;
  Heal the sick, the captive free,
  Let us all rejoice in thee!

HYMN XI.

THE SAME.

1 WE magnify thy grace, O Lord,
     How plent'ously hast thou prepar'd
     A supper for thy saints!
  All things are ready, thou hast said,
  A table thou hast richly spread,
     To answer all our wants.

2 Now, Lord, allure our souls to thee,
  O kindly bid us come and see,
     And taste how good thou art;
  Knock with the hammer of thy word,
  Knock by thy pow'rful Spirit, Lord,
     Lord, break into each heart!

3 Darkness and unbelief remove,
  Replenish all our souls with love,
     Cast out the power of sin;
  Jesus, attend our feeble pray'r,
  And for thyself our hearts prepare,
     Come in, dear Lord, come in.

B 2   4 Let

Let comfort, love, and joy, and peace,
  Like rivers flow, and ſtill increaſe,
    Unto the ocean driv'n:
Lord condeſcend to ſup with me
And grant I now may ſup with thee
    And ſup at laſt in heav'n!

HYMN XII.

TO THE TRINITY.

THE SAME.

1 COME thou almighty king,
  Help us thy name to ſing,
    Help us to praiſe!
Father all-glorious,
O'er all victorious,
Come, and reign over us
    ANTIENT OF DAYS.

2 Jeſus, our Lord ariſe,
  Scatter our enemies,
    And make them fall!
Let thine almighty aid
Our ſure defence be made—
Our ſouls on thee be ſtay'd—
    Lord hear our call!

3 Come, thou incarnate word,
   Gird on thy mighty sword—
      Our pray'r attend!
   Come! and thy people bless,
   And give thy word success,
   Spirit of holiness
      On us descend!

4 Come, holy comforter,
   Thy sacred witness bear
      In this glad hour!
   Thou who almighty art,
   Now rule in ev'ry heart,
   And ne'er from us depart,
      Spirit of pow'r!

5 To the great one in three
   Eternal praises be,
      Hence—evermore!
   His sov'reign majesty
   May we in glory see,
   And to eternity
      Love and adore.

HYMN XIII.

READING OR HEARING THE SCRIPTURES.

1 O God of wisdom, God of might,
   Great ruler in the realms of light;
  Whose truths are hid from prudent eyes,
  But make the babe and suckling wise;
Help thy unknowing servants, Lord,
To hear, and understand thy word.

2 Reveal thy scriptures to our mind,
   Here let us heav'nly treasures find;
  Do thou those sacred leaves unfold,
  Let us thy richest grace behold:
O let thy spirit lead us forth,
And teach us all its endless worth.

3 Direct us, left we judge amiss,
   Left error cloud the hidden bliss;
  Th' ingrafted word may we receive,
  And back to thee the glory give:
O make us know, O make us hear
The glorious tidings treasur'd there.

HYMN XIV.

UNFRUITFULNESS. ††

1 LONG have we sat beneath the sound
    Of thy salvation, Lord,
But still how weak our faith is found,
    And knowledge of thy word!

2 Oft we frequent thy holy place,
    Yet hear almost in vain;
How small a portion of thy grace
    Do our false hearts retain!

3 How cold and feeble is our love,
    How negligent our fear!
How low our hope of joys above,
    How few affections there!

4 Great God, thy sov'reign aid impart,
    To give thy word success;
Write thy salvation on our hearts,
    And make us learn thy grace.

5 Shew our forgetful feet the way,
    That leads to joys on high;
Where knowledge grows without decay,
    And love shall never die.

HYMN XV.

ANOTHER BEFORE SPEAKING.

1 GLORY to God, who gave the word,
    And bid the preachers cry;
Who caus'd his will to be proclaim'd,
    And brought salvation nigh.

2 Lord, ever give us of this bread,
    And grant us ears to hear;
Hearts to receive the heav'nly feed,
    And bring forth fruit with fear.

3 O may thy word direct our path,
    And guide our fault'ring feet;
Direct us in the living way,
    And to thy mercy-seat.

4 Fountain of everlasting life,
    Of bliss, and truth, and good;
Give us (that we may never thirst)
    To drink of Jesu's blood.

5 Fill every hungry soul, who cries,
    From thine exhaustless store;
And let no one go empty hence,
    But taste, and pray for more.

6 Let all thy children, Lord, be fed
  With the eternal word;
Be wise, and stronger grow thereby,
  Increasing in the Lord.

HYMN XVI.

AFTER SPEAKING.

1 WITH heart and lips unfeign'd,
   We praise thee for thy word;
 We bless thee for the joyful news
   Of our redeeming Lord.

2 Like as the kindly rain
   Returns not back to heav'n,
 But chears, and fruitful makes the earth,
   The end for which 'twas giv'n.

3 So let thy present voice
   Accomplish thy design;
 Distil on all our thirsty souls,
   And consecrate us thine.

4 Water thy sacred seed,
   And give it great increase;
 Let neither fowls, nor rocks, nor thorns,
   Hinder the fruits of peace.

5 Then

5 Then tho' we weeping sow,
   And tears our hours employ;
We know we shall return again,
   And bring our sheaves with joy.

6 Our lives now hid with Christ,
   With him shall soon appear;
And we array'd in all his light,
   Shall meet him in the air.

HYMN XVII.

MALACHI IV. 2.

1 O Sun of righteousness, arise,
   With healing in thy wing:
To my diseas'd, my fainting soul
   Thy free salvation bring.

2 All clouds of pride and sin-dispel
   By thine all-piercing beam;
Lighten mine eyes with faith, my heart
   With holy hope inflame.

3 My mind, by thy all-quick'ning pow'r,
   From vile desires set free,
Unite my scatter'd thoughts, and fix
   My love entire on thee.

4 Father,

4 Father, thy long-loſt child receive,
   Saviour thy purchaſe own;
Bleſt comforter, with peace and joy
   Thy waiting creature crown.

HYMN XVIII.

PANTING AFTER GOD.

1 THou hidden love of God, whoſe height,
      Whoſe depth unfathom'd no man knows;
   I ſee from far thy beauteous light,
      In'ly I ſigh for thy repoſe:
   My heart is pain'd, nor can it be
   At reſt, till it finds reſt in thee.

2 Is there a thing beneath the ſun,
      That ſtrives with thee, my heart, to ſhare?
   Ah! tear it thence, and reign alone,
      The Lord of every motion there:
   Then ſhall my heart from earth be free,
   When it has found repoſe in thee.

3 O hide this ſelf from me, that I
      No more, but Chriſt in me may live!
   My vile affections crucify,
      Let not one darling luſt ſurvive:
   In all things may I nothing ſee,
   Nothing deſire, or ſeek, but thee.

4 Each moment draw from earth away
    My heart, that lowly waits thy call;
Speak to my inmost soul, and say
    I am thy love, thy God, thy all!
To feel thy pow'r, to hear thy voice,
To taste thy love, be all my choice.

HYMN XIX.

A PRAYER FOR FAITH.

1 FATHER, I stretch my hands to thee,
      No other help I know;
  If thou withdraw thyself from me,
      Ah! whither shall I go?

2 What did thine only Son endure,
      Before I drew my breath?
  What pain, what labour to secure
      My soul from endless death!

3 O Jesu, cou'd I this believe,
      I now should feel thy pow'r;
  Now my poor soul thou would'st retrieve,
      Nor let me wait one hour.

4 Author of faith, to thee I lift
      My weary, longing eyes;
  O let me now receive that gift!
      My soul without it dies!

HYMN

HYMN XX.

ISAIAH IX. 2.

1 LIGHT of those, whose dreary dwelling
    Borders on the shades of death,
Come! and by thy love's revealing,
    Dissipate the clouds beneath:
The new heav'n and earth's creator,
    In our deepest darkness rise!
Scatt'ring all the light of nature,
    Pouring eye-sight on our eyes!

2 Still we wait for thine appearing
    Life and joy thy beams impart;
Chasing all our fears, and chearing
    Ev'ry poor benighted heart:
Come, and manifest the favour
    God hath for our ransom'd race;
Come, thou universal Saviour,
    Come, and bring thy gospel-grace.

3 Save us in thy great compassion,
    O thou mild pacific prince!
Give the knowledge of salvation,
    Give the pardon of our sin!
By thine all-restoring merit,
    Ev'ry burthen'd soul release,
Ev'ry weary, wand'ring spirit
    Guide into thy perfect peace.

HYMN XXI.

ZECHARIAH XIII. I.

1 HOW sad our state by nature is,
    Our sin how deep it stains!
And Satan binds our captive souls
    Fast in his slavish chains.

2 But there's a voice of sov'reign grace
    Sounds from God's sacred word;
Ho! ye despairing sinners, come
    And trust upon the Lord.

3 O may we hear th' Almighty call,
    And run to this relief;
We wou'd believe thy promise, Lord,
    O help our unbelief!

4 To the blest fountain of thy blood,
    Teach us, O Lord! to fly:
There may we wash our spotted souls!
    From crimes of deepest dye!

5 Stretch out thine arm, victorious king,
    Our reigning sins subdue;
Drive the old dragon from his seat,
    And form our souls anew.

6 Poor guilty, weak, and helpless worms,
   On thy kind arm we fall;
Be thou our strength and righteousness,
   Our Jesus and our all.

HYMN XXII.

ISAIAH XL. 29.

1 SON of God thy blessing grant,
   Still supply my ev'ry want;
Tree of life! thine influ'nce shed,
With thy sap my spirit feed.

2 Tend'rest branch, alas! am I,
With'ring without thee, lo! I die;
Weak as helpless infancy,
O confirm my soul in thee!

3 Unsustain'd by thee, I fall,
Send the strength for which I call!
Weaker than a bruised reed,
Help I ev'ry moment need.

4 All my hopes on thee depend,
Love me, save me to the end!
Give me the continuing grace;
Take th' everlasting praise!

HYMN XXIII.

MIRACLES APPLIED.

1 O Lord! to whom for help I call,
    Thy miracles repeat;
With pitying eye behold me fall
    A leper at thy feet.

2 Loathsome, and foul, and, self-abhorr'd,
    I sink beneath my sin;
But, if thou wilt, a gracious word
    Of thine can make me clean.

3 Thou seest me deaf to thy commands,
    Open, O Lord! mine ear;
Bid me stretch out my wither'd hands,
    And lift them up in pray'r.

4 Silent (alas! thou know'st how long!)
    My voice I cannot raise;
But, O! when thou shalt loose my tongue,
    The dumb shall sing thy praise.

5 Lame at the pool I still am found,
    Give, and my strength employ;
Light as an hart I then shall bound,
    The lame shall leap for joy.

6 Blind from my birth to guilt and thee,
    And dark I am within;
  The love of God I cannot see,
    Nor sinfulness of sin.

7 But thou, they say, art passing by,
    O let me find thee near!
  Jesus, in mercy hear my cry,
    Thou son of David, hear!

8 Long have I waited in the way,
    For thee, the heav'nly light;
  Command me to be brought, and say,
    " Sinner, receive thy sight."

HYMN XXIV.

THE SAME.

1 JESU, Redeemer, Saviour, **Lord,**
    The weary sinner's friend;
  Come to my help, pronounce the word,
    Bid my corruptions end.

2 Thou canst o'ercome this heart of mine,
    Thou canst victorious prove;
  For everlasting strength is thine,
    And everlasting love.

3 Thy pow'rful spirit can subdue
   Unconquerable sin;
Cleanse my foul heart, and make it new,
   And write thy law within.

4 Bound down with twice ten thousand ties,
   Yet let me hear thy call;
My soul in confidence shall rise,
   Shall rise and break thro' all.

5 Speak, and the deaf shall hear thy voice,
   The blind his sight receive,
The dumb in songs of praise rejoice,
   The heart of stone believe.

6 The Æthiop then shall change his skin,
   The dead shall feel thy pow'r;
The loathsome leper shall be clean,
   And I shall sin abhor.

HYMN XXV.

SPIRITUAL BARRENNESS.

1 MOST righteous God, my doom I bear,
   My load of guilt, my pain and care,
Inslav'd to base desires;
Hard toiling for imbitter'd bread,
I mourn my barren soul o'erspread
   With cursed thorns and briars.

2 Death's sentence in myself receive,
 And dust to dust already cleave,
  Exil'd from paradise;
 Hast'ning to hellish misery,
 Jesus, if unredeem'd by thee,
  My soul for ever dies!

3 But Jesus hath my sentence borne,
 He did in my affliction mourn,
  A man of sorrows made;
 A servant and a curse for me,
 He bore the utmost penalty,
  He suffer'd in my stead.

4 I see him sweat great drops of blood,
 I see him faint beneath my load!
  The thorns his temples tear!
 He bows his bleeding head and dies!
 He lives! he mounts above the skies!
  He claims my Eden there!

HYMN XXVI.

FOR FAITH.

1 AUTHOR of true and saving faith,
  That grace to me impart;
 Grant me an int'rest in thy death,
  A new believing heart.

2 Dismiss

2 Dismiss my griefs, my sorrows end,
 My reas'ning's voice controul;
Lord, shew thyself a sinner's friend,
 And bless my helpless soul.

3 At times thy word's attracting beams
 Have drawn my soul above;
Diffusing thro' my heart the streams
 Of everlasting love.

4 Sometimes I've had a little taste,
 And thought thy coming nigh;
But ah! the blessing did not last,
 The visitant pass'd by.

5 And must I ever mourning go,
 A stranger to thy love;
Shall I be join'd with saints below,
 And not with saints above?

6 Shall I beneath the gospel stay,
 And hear the call of grace;
And at the awful judgment-day
 Be banish'd from thy face?

7 Lord, grant me to believe in hope,
 That soon thou wilt me bless;
And at the last wilt raise me up,
 A kingdom to possess.

HYMN

HYMN XXVII.

FOR A CLEAN HEART.

1 O For an heart to love my God!
    An heart from sin set free;
An heart that always feels the blood,
    So freely shed for me!

2 An heart resign'd, submissive, meek,
    My dear redeemer's throne;
Where only Christ is heard to speak,
    Where Jesus reigns alone.

3 An humble, lowly, contrite heart,
    Believing, true and clean;
Which neither life nor death can part
    From him that dwells within.

4 An heart in every thought renew'd,
    And fill'd with love divine:
Perfect and right, and pure, and good,
    A copy, Lord! of thine.

5 Thy tender heart is still the same,
    And melts at human woe;
Send down thy grace, O blessed Lamb!
    That I thy love may know.

6 Thy holy nature, Lord! impart,
   Come quickly from above;
Write thy new name upon my heart,
   Thy new beſt name of love.

HYMN XXVIII.

LONGING AFTER GOD.

1 GReat God! indulge my humble claim,
   Be thou my joy, my hope, my reſt;
The glories that compoſe thy name,
   Stand all engag'd to make me bleſt!

2 Thou great and good, thou juſt and wiſe,
   Be thou my father, and my God!
And make me thine by ſacred ties,
   Thy ſon, thy ſervant bought with blood.

3 With heart, and eyes, and lifted hands,
   For thee I long, to thee I look;
As trav'lers do in thirſty lands
   Pant for the cooling water-brook.

4 O may thy love inſpire my tongue,
   Salvation ſhall be all my ſong;
And all my pow'rs ſhall join to bleſs
   The Lord my ſtrength and righteouſneſs.

HYMN XXIX.

THE POOR SINNER.

1 GOD of my salvation, hear,
    And help me to believe;
Simply do I now draw near,
    Thy blessing to receive:
Full of guilt, alas! I am,
    But to thy wounds for refuge flee;
Friend of sinners, spotless Lamb,
    Thy blood was shed for me.

2 Nothing have I, Lord, to pay,
    Nor can thy grace procure;
Empty send me not away,
    For I, thou know'st am poor;
Dust and ashes is my name,
    My all is sin and misery:
Friend of sinners, spotless Lamb,
    Thy blood was shed for me.

3 Without money, without price,
    I come thy love to buy;
From myself I turn my eyes,
    The chief of sinners, I:
Take, O take me, as I am,
    And let me lose myself in thee;
Friend of sinners, spotless Lamb,
    Thy blood was shed for me.

HYMN XXX.

THE SAME.

1 JESU, friend of sinners, hear,
  Yet once again, I pray;
From my debt of sin set clear,
  For I have nought to pay.
Speak, O speak the kind release,
  A poor backsliding soul restore;
Love me freely, seal my peace,
  And bid me sin no more.

2 Sin's deceitfulness hath spread
  An hardness o'er my heart;
But if thou thy spirit shed,
  The stony shall depart:
Shed thy love, thy tenderness,
  And let me feel thy soft'ning pow'r;
Love me freely, seal my peace,
  And bid me sin no more.

3 For this only thing, I pray,
  And this will I require,
Take the pow'r of sin away,
  Take ev'ry vain desire:
Perfect me in holiness,
  Thine image to my soul restore;
Love me freely, seal my peace,
  And bid me sin no more.

HYMN XXXI.

TO JESUS CHRIST.

1 JESU, Jesu, king of saints,
　Known to thee are all my wants;
　Self-convicted, self-abhorr'd,
　I approach thee, dearest Lord.

2 Known to thee, whose eyes are flame,
　I thy love and pity claim;
　With an eye of love look down,
　Help, Lord, help me very soon.

3 Still I feel a fleshly part,
　Much corruption in my heart;
　Oh! I'm very vile indeed,
　Of thy blood I sure have need.

4 Break, O break this heart of stone,
　Form it for thy use alone;
　Bid each vanity depart,
　Build thy temple in my heart.

5 This be my support in need,
　That thou didst so freely bleed;
　Hence my hopes and joys arise,
　From thy bloody sacrifice.

6 This confirms me when I'm weak,
  Comforts me when I'm sick;
  Gives me courage when I faint,
  Well supplies my ev'ry want.

7 Saviour to my heart be near,
  Exercise the shepherd's care;
  Guard my weakness by thy grace,
  Let me feel a constant peace.

HYMN XXXII.

THE SAME.

1 GRound, O ground me on the Lamb,
    Other Saviours I disclaim;
  Fix my heart on thee to stay,
  Do it, Lord, without delay.

2 Empty is created good,
  I want more substantial food;
  All is vanity beside
  Jesus, and him crucify'd.

3 Fruitless is my search to find
  True serenity of mind,
  Till I have with Jesus been,
  And his smiling face have seen.

4 In thy presence may I dwell,
　Subject to thy holy will;
　Show'r on me thy pow'r divine,
　Mortify the man of sin.

5 While I traverse here on earth,
　Thy kind influ'nce on me breathe;
　Reconcil'd to me appear,
　And thy righteousness bring near.

6 Grant me still in grace to grow,
　While a pilgrim here below;
　Let me by thy Spirit move,
　And with all my heart thee love.

HYMN XXXIII.

HUMAN WEAKNESS.

1 JESUS, vouchsafe to hear the cry,
　　Of a poor feeble heart;
　Reach out thy hand, and draw me nigh,
　　Nor let me thence depart.

2 My state deplorable appears,
　　Clearly the same I see;
　But yet, alas! can shed no tears,
　　Nor feel my misery.

3 Beneath thy word, the gospel-word,
  Careless and cold I sit;
My heart is hard, extremely hard,
  Dear Jesus, soften it.

4 To others, Lord, thou dost convey,
  Thy chearing beams, when crav'd;
And must I ever go away
  Empty, and unreliev'd?

5 Thunder upon my heart, dear Lord,
  And make each corner shake,
That I may melt beneath thy word,
  And of thy bliss partake.

6 Lord, give me patience, give me more,
  Until that hour appear,
When I in heart can thee adore,
  And feel thy presence there.

HYMN XXXIV.

THE SAME.

1 DEAR Lord, attend my pray'r,
    And all my wants relieve;
  Come to my heart, and dwell thou there,
    That thou in me may'st live.

2   In weakness I draw nigh
      Unto the throne of grace:
   Answer the sinner's mournful cry,
      And fill me with thy peace.

3   Thou read'st my naked breast,
      For liberty I groan;
   I sigh in thee, my Lord, to rest,
      And worship thee alone.

4   Fain would I hate my sin,
      And ponder on thy love;
   'Till all be sanctify'd within,
      And my whole heart's above.

5   If trials vex my mind,
      Close to thy wounds I'll flee;
   No refuge may I elsewhere find,
      No refuge but in thee.

6   To thee I recommend
      My poor and trembling soul;
   On thee for future grace depend,
      Who art my all in all.

HYMN XXXV.

MEEKNESS AND HUMILITY.

1 LORD, if thou the grace impart,
    Poor in spirit, meek in heart;
I shall as my master be,
Rooted in humility.

2 From the time that thee I know,
Nothing wou'd I seek below;
Aim at nothing great or high,
Lowly both in heart and eye.

3 Simple, teachable, and mild,
Chang'd into a little child;
Pleas'd with all the Lord provides,
Wean'd from all the world besides.

4 Father, fix my soul on thee,
Ev'ry evil let me flee;
Nothing want beneath, above,
Happy in thy precious love.

5 O! that all may seek, and find
Every good in Jesus join'd!
Him let Israel still adore,
Trust him, praise him evermore.

HYMN XXXVI.

PSALM V.

1 ON thee, O God of purity,
    I wait for hallowing grace;
None without holiness shall see
    The glories of thy face:
In souls unholy, and unclean,
    Thou never canst delight;
Nor shall they, while unsav'd from sin,
    Appear before thy sight.

2 But as for me, with humble fear,
    I will approach thy gate;
Though most unworthy to draw near,
    Or in thy courts to wait:
I trust in thine unbounded grace,
    To all so freely given;
And worship t'ward thine holy place,
    And lift my soul to heav'n.

3 Lead me in all thy righteous ways,
    Nor suffer me to slide;
Point out the path before my face,
    My God, be thou my guide!
O may I ne'er to evil yield,
    Defended from above,
And kept, and cover'd with the shield
    Of thine almighty love.

HYMN XXXVII.

BREATHING AFTER HOLINESS.

1 O That the Lord wou'd guide my ways,
    To keep his statutes still!
O that my God would give me grace,
    To know, and do his will!

2 Lord, send thy Spirit down to write
    Thy law upon my heart!
Nor let my tongue indulge deceit,
    Nor act a liar's part.

3 From vanity, Lord, turn mine eyes,
    Let no corrupt design,
No covetous desires arise
    Within this soul of mine.

4 Order my footsteps by thy word,
    And make my heart sincere;
Let sin have no dominion, Lord,
    But keep my conscience clear.

5 My soul hath gone too far astray,
    My feet too often slip;
I would not, Lord! forget thy way,
    Bring back the wand'ring sheep.

6 Make me to walk in thy commands,
   'Tis a delightful road;
 Nor let my head, my heart, or hands,
   Offend against my God.

HYMN XXXVIII.

PREVENTING GRACE.

OFT' hast thou, Lord, in tender love,
   Prevented my request,
 And sent thy Spirit from above,
   An unexpected guest.

2 Oft' when my pray'r was scarce begun,
   Thou didst thy grace impart,
 And make thy pard'ning mercy known,
   And seal it on my heart.

3 Why this profusion of thy grace
   On such a worm as me?
 Father, I ask, in fixt amaze,
   Explain the mystery.

4 How can'st thou to a sinner's cry
   Incline thy pitying ear?
 Thou hear'st mine advocate on high,
   And wilt for ever hear.

HYMN XXXIX.

LUKE X. 39.

1 THE one thing needful, that good part,
    Which Mary chose with all her heart,
I wou'd pursue with heart and mind,
And seek unweary'd till I find.

2 But, oh! I'm blind and ignorant,
The Spirit of the Lord I want;
To guide me in the narrow road,
That leads to happiness and God.

3 O Lord, my God, to thee I pray,
Teach me to know, and find the way
How I may have my sins forgiv'n,
And safe, and surely get to heav'n.

4 My mind enlighten with thy light,
That I may understand aright
The glorious gospel-myst'ry,
Which shews the way to heav'n and thee.

5 Hidden in Christ the treasure lies,
That goodly pearl of so great price;
No other way but Christ, there is
To endless happiness and bliss.

6 O Jesus Christ, my Lord and God,
  Who hast redeem'd me by thy blood;
  Unite my heart so fast to thee,
  That we may never parted be.

HYMN XL.

A SINNER's PRAYER.

1 WHEN, gracious Lord, when shall it be,
    That I shall find my all in thee;
  The fulness of thy promise prove,
  The seal of thine eternal love?

2 Thee, only thee I fain wou'd find,
  And cast the world and flesh behind;
  An helpless soul I come to thee,
  With only sin and misery.

3 Lord I am sick, my sickness cure;
  I want, do thou enrich the poor:
  Under thy mighty hand I stoop,
  O lift the abject sinner up.

4 Lord, I am blind, be thou my sight;
  Lord, I am weak, be thou my might;
  An helper of the helpless be,
  And let me find my all in thee.

HYMN XLI.

THE SAME.

1 O My Lord, what muſt I do?
   Only thou the way canſt ſhew;
Thou canſt ſave me in this hour,
I have neither will nor pow'r:
God if over all thou art,
Greater than the ſinful heart;
Let it now on me be ſhown,
Take away the heart of ſtone.

2 Take away my darling ſin,
Make me willing to be clean;
Make me willing to receive
What thy goodneſs waits to give:
Force me, Lord, with all to part,
Tear all idols from my heart;
All thy pow'r on me be ſhewn,
Take away the heart of ſtone.

3 Jeſu, mighty to renew,
Work in me to will and do;
Turn my nature's rapid tide,
Stem the torrent of my pride,
Stop the whirlwind of my will,
Bid corruptions, Lord, be ſtill;
Now thy love almighty ſhew,
Make e'en me a creature new.

4 Arm of God, thy strength put on,
Bow the heavens, and come down;
All mine unbelief o'erthrow,
Lay th' aspiring mountain low;
Conquer thy worst foe in me,
Get thyself the victory,
Save the vilest of the race,
Force me to be sav'd by grace.

HYMN XLII.

DESIRING CHRIST.

1 COME, O thou universal good!
Balm of the wounded conscience, come!
The hungry, dying spirit's food,
The weary wand'ring pilgrim's home;
Haven to take the shipwreck'd in,
My everlasting rest from sin!

2 Come, O my comfort and delight!
My strength and health, my shield and sun,
My boast, my confidence, and might,
My joy, my glory, and my crown;
My gospel-hope, my calling's prize,
My tree of life, my paradise.

HYMN XLIII.

THE PRESSURE OF SIN.

1 O That my load of sin were gone!
    O that I cou'd at last submit,
At Jesu's feet to lay it down,
    To lay my soul at Jesu's feet!

2 When shall mine eyes behold the Lamb,
    The God of my salvation see!
Weary, O Lord, thou know'st I am,
    Yet still I cannot come to thee.

3 Rest for my soul I long to find,
    Saviour, if mine indeed thou art,
Give me thy meek and lowly mind,
    And stamp thine image on my heart.

4 I wou'd, but thou must give the pow'r,
    My heart from ev'ry sin release;
Bring near, bring near the joyful hour,
    And fill me with thy heav'nly peace.

5 Come, Lord, the drooping sinner chear,
    Let not my Jesus long delay;
Appear, in my poor heart appear,
    My God, my Saviour, come away!

HYMN XLIV.

AN HUMBLE HOPE.

1 O What shall I do my Saviour to praise,
   So faithful and true, so plenteous in grace,
  So strong to deliver, so good to redeem
  The weakest believer, that hangs upon him.

2 How happy the man, whose heart is set free,
  The people that can be joyful in thee!
  Their joy is to walk in the light of thy face,
  And still they are talking of Jesus's grace.

3 Their daily delight shall be in thy name;
  They shall as their right thy righteousness claim,
  Thy righteousness wearing, and cleans'd by thy blood,
  Bold shall they appear in the presence of God.

4 For thou art their boast, their glory and pow'r,
  And I also trust to see the glad hour,
  My soul's new creation, a life from the dead,
  The day of salvation, that lifts up my head.

E 2   5 Yes,

5 Yes, Lord, I shall see the bliss of thine own,
Thy secret to me shall soon be made known;
For sorrow and sadness, I joy shall receive,
And share in the gladness of all that believe.

HYMN XLV.

THE VOICE OF CHRIST.

1 THE voice of my beloved sounds
   Over the rocks, and rising grounds;
O'er hills of guilt, and seas of grief,
He leaps, he flies to my relief.

2 Now thro' the veil of flesh I see,
With eyes of love he looks on me;
Now in the gospel's clearest glass,
He shews the beauties of his face.

3 Gently he draws my heart along
Both with his beauties, and his tongue;
Rise, saith my Lord, and come away,
No mortal joys are worth thy stay.

4 Lo! glad I come, and thou blest Lamb
Shalt take me to thee as I am;
Nothing but sin I thee can give,
Nothing but love shall I receive.

HYMN XLVI.

HUMILIATION.

1 SHEW pity, Lord, O Lord forgive,
   Let a repenting rebel live;
   Are not thy mercies large and free?
   May not a sinner trust in thee?

2 My crimes are great, but don't surpass
   The pow'r and glory of thy grace;
   Great God, thy nature hath no bound,
   So let thy pard'ning love be found.

3 O wash my soul from every sin,
   And make my guilty conscience clean;
   Here on my heart the burthen lies,
   And past offences pain my eyes.

4 My lips with shame, my sins confess,
   Against thy law, against thy grace;
   Lord, should thy judgment grow severe,
   I am condemn'd, but thou art clear.

5 Yet save a trembling sinner, Lord,
   Whose hope, still hov'ring round thy word,
   Wou'd light on some sweet promise there,
   Some sure support against despair.

HYMN XLVII.

THE SAME.

PSALM LI.

1 O Thou that hear'ft when finners cry,
   Tho' all my crimes before thee lie;
Behold me not with angry look,
But blot their mem'ry from thy book.

2 I cannot live without thy light,
Caft out and banifh'd from thy fight;
Thy faving-grace, O Lord, reftore,
And guard me that I fall no more.

3 Though I have griev'd thy fpirit, Lord,
It's help and comfort ftill afford;
And let a wretch come near thy throne,
To plead the merits of thy fon.

4 My foul lies humbled in the duft,
And owns thy awful fentence juft;
Look down, O Lord, with pitying eye,
And fave a foul condemn'd to die.

5 Then will I teach the world thy ways,
Sinners fhall learn thy fov'reign grace;
I'll lead them to my Saviour's blood,
And they fhall praife a pard'ning God.

HYMN XLVIII.

THE SAME.

1 LORD, I am vile, conceiv'd in sin,
 And born unholy, and unclean;
 Sprung from the man, whose guilty fall
 Corrupts the race, and taints us all.

2 Soon as we draw our infant-breath,
 The seeds of sin grow up for death;
 Thy law demands a perfect heart,
 But we're defil'd in ev'ry part.

3 Great God, create my heart anew,
 And form my spirit pure and true;
 O make me wise betimes to spy
 My danger, and my remedy.

4 Behold I fall before thy face,
 My only refuge is thy grace;
 No outward forms can make me clean,
 The leprosy lies deep within.

5 Jesus, my God, thy blood alone
 Hath pow'r sufficient to atone;
 Thy blood can make me white as snow,
 No other thing can cleanse me so.

6 While guilt disturbs and breaks my peace,
Nor flesh, nor soul hath rest or ease;
Lord let me hear thy pard'ning voice,
And make my broken heart rejoice.

HYMN XLIX.

THE SAME.

1 LORD, I would spread my sore distress,
   And guilt before thine eyes;
Against thy laws, against thy grace,
   How high my crimes arise!

2 I from the stock of Adam came,
   Unholy, and unclean;
All my original is shame,
   And all my nature sin.

3 Born in a world of guilt, I drew
   Contagion with my breath;
And as my days advanc'd, I grew
   A juster prey for death.

4 Cleanse me, O Lord, and chear my soul
   With thy forgiving love;
O make my broken spirit whole,
   And make my sins remove.

5 Let

5 Let not thy spirit quite depart,
    Nor drive me from thy face;
Create anew my vicious heart,
    And fill it with thy grace.

6 Then will I make thy mercy known
    Before the sons of men;
Backsliders shall address thy throne,
    And turn to God again.

HYMN L.

FOR SERIOUSNESS.

1 THOU God of glorious majesty!
    To thee, against myself, to thee,
        A worm of earth I cry:
An half awaken'd child of man,
An heir of endless bliss or pain,
        A sinner born to die.

2 Lo! on a narrow neck of land,
'Twixt two unbounded seas I stand,
        Secure—insensible!
A point of time, a moment's space,
Removes me to that heav'nly place,
        Or shuts me up in hell.

3 O God, mine inmoſt ſoul convert!
And deeply on my thoughtful heart,
   Eternal things impreſs;
Give me to feel their ſolemn weight,
And tremble on the brink of fate,
   And 'wake to righteouſneſs.

4 Before me place in dread array,
The pomp of that tremendous day.
   When thou with clouds ſhalt come,
To judge the nations at thy bar,
And tell me, Lord! ſhall I be there,
   To meet a joyful doom!

5 Be this my one great buſ'neſs here,
With ſerious induſtry and fear,
   My future bliſs t'enſure!
Thine utmoſt council to fulfil,
And ſuffer all thy righteous will,
   And to the end endure.

6 Then, Saviour, then my ſoul receive,
Tranſported from the vale to live,
   And reign with thee above;
Where faith is ſweetly loſt in ſight,
And hope in full ſupreme delight,
   And everlaſting love.

HYMN LI.

FOR A BELIEVER.

1 HOW, my dear Lord, shall I express
　　The present happiness I share?
With joy my heart can now confess
　　That Jesu's name is written there.

2 I, who on husks but lately fed,
　　A prodigal estrang'd from God,
Now eat the true and heav'nly bread,
　　And feed on more than angel's food.

3 Christ holds me in his arms of grace,
　　And marks me for his blood-bought one;
And I thro' faith beholds his face,
　　And feels I'm his adopted son.

4 Sunk in love's bottomless abyss,
　　With saints and angels now I join;
I cannot but my Lord caress,
　　In melody and songs divine.

5 Yet still I only thirst, while here
　　The happy life of faith to live;
More choice, and riper fruits to bear,
　　Till I on Sion's shore arrive.

6 Let me purſue the path begun,
　　Gladly therein my days to ſpend;
　Till all my pilgrimage is done,
　　And faith, and hope in glory end.

HYMN LII.

THE DAY OF ESPOUSALS.

1 Sweet was the hour, the minutes ſweet,
　When my beloved me did meet,
　　His death to evidence:
My heart, which wounded was before,
Kindly he bound; therein did pour
　　Love's healing quinteſſence.

2 Death's heritage he then laid waſte,
　And calm'd each ſtormy furious blaſt,
　　And cancel'd all my ſins;
Placing his croſs before my eyes,
Look to me, and be ſav'd, he cries,
　　From death thy life begins.

3 Sweet was the feaſt my heart enjoy'd,
　I ate, I drank, nor was I cloy'd,
　　For more I thirſted ſtill:
Here let me ſtay, I longing pray'd,
Sure this is Achor's vale, I ſaid,
　　Or holy Tabor's hill.

4 His left hand under me was plac'd,
   And his right hand my soul embrac'd,
      His kindness sweet did prove:
   Safely I sat beneath his shade,
   Quite round my soul he overspread
      His canopy of love.

5 I sung assur'd of Jesu's love,
   Refresh'd with manna from above,
      For flesh no more I cry'd:
   Warm'd with the sun's enliv'ning beams,
   I laid me down at Shiloh's streams,
      Content and satisfy'd.

6 Untouch'd by Satan's envious crew,
   Upon my fleece, like drops of dew,
      His free grace did descend:
   Strangers in vain attempt to tell
   The joy immense, unspeakable,
      I found in Christ my friend.

7 Thus free'd from bondage, I did prove
   The sweets of his redeeming love,
      And bask'd in sunny beams:
   In this sweet frame may I rejoice,
   Still hearken to my Saviour's voice,
      Still drink those living streams!

HYMN LIII.

THE PETITION.

1 O Deareſt Lord, give me an heart,
    Inflam'd with love to thee;
That thro' thy tedious toil and ſmart,
    My ſoul may happy be.

2 I want, O Lord, from ſin to flee,
    And in thy wounds to reſt;
Bid me by faith come near to thee,
    And lean upon thy breaſt.

3 Still let a ſenſe of what thou'ſt done,
    In my hard heart be felt;
That by the love to me thou'ſt ſhewn,
    My inmoſt ſoul may melt.

4 O may I never, never faint,
    Refreſh'd by ſtreams of love;
'Till in thy glory as a ſaint,
    I live with thoſe above.

5 O may I now my all give up,
    To thee, my deareſt Lord;
And wait with all thy ſaints to ſup
    Around the feſtal board.

HYMN LIV.

CHRIST PRECIOUS TO A BELIEVER.

1 JESUS, I love thy charming name,
  'Tis music to my ear;
Fain wou'd I sound it out so loud,
  That earth and heav'n might hear.

2 Yes, thou art precious to my soul,
  My transport, and my trust;
Jewels to thee are gaudy toys,
  And gold is sordid dust.

3 All my capacious pow'rs can wish
  In thee most richly meet;
Nor to my eyes is life so dear,
  Nor friendship half so sweet.

4 O may thy grace still chear my heart!
  And shed its fragrance there!
The noblest balm of all its wounds,
  The cordial of its care.

5 I'll speak the honours of thy name
  With my last lab'ring breath;
When speechless, clasp thee in my arms,
  My joy in life and death!

HYMN LV.

PRAISE TO CHRIST.

1 COME let us join our chearful songs,
    With angels round the throne;
Ten thousand thousand are their tongues,
    But all their joys are one.

2 Worthy the Lamb that dy'd, they cry,
    To be exalted thus;
Worthy the Lamb, our lips reply,
    For he was slain for us.

3 Jesus is worthy to receive
    Honour and pow'r divine;
And blessings more than we can give,
    Be, Lord, for ever thine.

4 Let all that dwell above the sky,
    And air, and earth, and seas;
Conspire to lift thy glories high,
    And speak thine endless praise.

5 Let all creation join in one,
    To bless the sacred name
Of him, that sits upon the throne,
    And to adore the lamb.

HYMN LVI.

CHRIST OUR WISDOM.

1 HOW heavy is the night,
    That hangs upon our eyes;
'Till Christ with his reviving light,
    Upon our souls arise?

2 Our guilty spirits dread
    To meet the wrath of heav'n;
But in his righteousness array'd,
    We see our sins forgiv'n.

3 Unholy, and impure
    Are all our thoughts and ways;
His hands infected nature cure,
    With sanctifying grace.

4 The pow'rs of hell agree
    To hold our souls in vain;
He sets the sons of bondage free,
    And breaks the cursed chain.

5 Lord, we adore thy ways,
    To bring us near to God;
Thy sov'reign pow'r, thy healing grace,
    And thine atoning blood.

HYMN LVIII.

CHRIST's COMPASSION TO THE TEMPTED.

1 WITH joy we meditate the grace
Of our high-prieſt above;
His heart is made of tenderneſs,
His bowels melt with love.

2 Touch'd with a ſympathy within,
He knows our feeble frame;
He knows what ſore temptations mean,
For he hath felt the ſame.

3 He in the days of feeble fleſh
Pour'd out ſtrong cries and tears;
And in his meaſure feels afreſh,
What ev'ry member bears.

4 He'll never quench the ſmoaking flax
But raiſe it to a flame;
The bruiſed reed he never breaks,
Nor ſcorns the meaneſt name.

5 Then let our humble faith addreſs
His mercy, and his pow'r;
We ſhall obtain deliv'ring grace,
In the diſtreſſing hour.

HYMN LVIII.

LOVE.

1 HAPPY the heart, where graces reign,
    Where love inspires the breast;
Love is the brightest of the train,
    And perfects all the rest.

2 Knowledge, alas! 'tis all in vain,
    And all in vain our fear;
Our stubborn sins will fight and reign,
    If love be absent there.

3 'Tis love that makes our chearful feet
    In swift obedience move;
The devils know, and tremble too,
    But Satan cannot love.

4 This is the grace that lives and sings,
    When faith and hope shall cease;
'Tis this shall strike our joyful strings,
    In the sweet realms of bliss.

5 When join'd to that harmonious throng,
    That fills the choirs above;
Then shall we tune our golden harps,
    And ev'ry note be love.

HYMN LIX.

LIGHT IN DARKNESS.

1 MY God, the spring of all my joys,
    The life of my delights;
The glory of my brightest days,
    And comfort of my nights!

2 In darkest shades if thou appear,
    My dawning is begun!
Thou art my soul's bright morning-star,
    And thou my rising sun.

3 The op'ning heav'ns around me shine
    With beams of sacred bliss,
When Jesus shews his mercy's mine,
    And whispers, I AM HIS.

4 My soul cou'd leave this heavy clay,
    At that transporting word;
Run up with joy the shining way
    To meet and praise my Lord.

5 Fearless of hell and ghastly death,
    I'd break thro' ev'ry foe;
The wings of love, and arms of faith,
    Shall bear me conqu'ror through.

HYMN LX.

CHRIST's LOVE UNIVERSAL.

1 THE Saviour's love once truly known,
    The man of sin, and self pulls down;
 Humbles the sinner at his feet,
 And makes his wounds and passion sweet.

2 Bow'd down in shame we gladly own
 The work to be the Lord's alone;
 To him our very all we owe,
 What of ourselves, or God, we know.

3 Our works no longer then we praise,
 Nothing extol but Jesu's grace;
 Free and unmerited we prove
 The boundless height and depth of love.

4 While thus we learn the needful part,
 Shame fills, love warms the grateful heart;
 While on his suff'ring form we muse,
 Our cares, and very thoughts we lose.

5 We stand amaz'd, and wonder why
 The Saviour cou'd for sinners die;
 We blush to see him in his blood;
 Yet here we look, and drop our load.

6 Then

6 Then, O my soul, how canst thou be
So cold to him, who dy'd for thee?
All blessings from the cross proceed,
Look there, my soul, in all thy need.

HYMN LXI.

PHIL. IV. 4.

1 REJOICE the Lord is king,
    Your God and king adore;
Mortals give thanks, and sing,
    And triumph evermore:
Lift up your hearts, lift up your voice,
Rejoice, again I say, rejoice.

2 Jesus the Saviour reigns,
    The God of truth and love;
When he had purg'd our stains,
    He took his seat above:
Lift up your hearts, lift up your voice,
Rejoice, again I say, rejoice.

3 His kingdom cannot fail,
    He rules o'er earth and heav'n;
The keys of death and hell
    Are to our Jesus giv'n:
Lift up your hearts, lift up your voice,
Rejoice, again I say, rejoice.

4 He sits at God's right hand,
   'Till all his foes submit,
And bow to his command,
   And fall beneath his feet:
Lift up your hearts, lift up your voice,
Rejoice, again I say, rejoice.

5 He all his foes shall quell,
   Shall all our sins destroy,
And ev'ry bosom swell
   With pure seraphic joy:
Lift up your hearts, lift up your voice,
Rejoice, again I say, rejoice.

6 Rejoice in glorious hope,
   Jesus the judge shall come,
And take his servants up,
   To their eternal home:
We soon shall hear th' archangel's voice,
The trump of God shall sound, rejoice.

HYMN LXII.

THE BELIEVER's REQUEST.

1 JESUS, the Saviour of my soul,
   Be thou my heart's delight;
Remain the same to me alway,
   My joy by day and night.

2 Hungry and thirsty after thee
    May I be found each hour;
  Humble in heart, and happy kept,
    By thy almighty pow'r.

3 O may I never once forget
    What a poor worm I am;
  From death and hell redeem'd by blood,
    The blood of God's dear lamb.

4 May thy blest spirit in my heart,
    Sweetly diffuse abroad
  The love of God, th'incarnate God,
    Who bought me with his blood.

5 In holy reverence I wou'd
    With all my heart retain
  Th' atonement made by Jesu's blood,
    And all his wounds and pain.

6 The myst'ry of redeeming love,
    Be ever dear to me;
  And may the flesh and blood of Christ
    My choicest dainty be.

HYMN LXIII.

REJOICE EVERMORE.

1 REJOICE evermore,
    With angels above,
In Jesus's power,
    In Jesus's love;
With glad exultation
    Your triumph proclaim,
Ascribing salvation
    To God and the Lamb.

2 Thou, Lord, our relief
    In trouble hast been,
Hast sav'd us from grief,
    Hast sav'd us from sin;
The pow'r of thy spirit
    Can set our hearts free;
And we shall inherit
    All fulness in thee.

3 All fulness of peace,
    All fulness of joy,
And spiritual bliss
    That never can cloy:
To us it is given
    In Jesus to know,
A kingdom of heaven,
    An heaven below.

4   No longer we join
      Where sinners invite,
    Or envy the swine
      Their brutish delight;
    Their joy is all sadness,
      Their mirth is all vain;
    Their laughter is madness,
      Their pleasure is pain.

5   O may they at last
      With sorrow return,
    The pleasure to taste
      For which they were born!
    Our Jesus receiving,
      Our happiness prove,
    The joy of believing,
      The heaven of love.

HYMN LXIV.

1 LO! to the hills I lift mine eyes,
      Thy promis'd help I claim;
    Father of mercies, glorify
      The holy Jesu's name.

2 Salvation in that name is found,
      Balm of my grief and care;
    A medicine for my ev'ry wound,
      All, all I want is there.

HYMN LXV.

CHRIST OUR ONLY REFUGE.

1 HOW bleft are they, whofe feet have found
The way unto Immanuel's ground;
And ftedfaftly do walk therein,
Far from the crooked paths of fin!

2 Their weary fpirits fweetly reft
Contentedly on Jefu's breaft;
They fo much of his mercy prove,
As that they cannot help but love.

3 In peace their hearts enjoy the Lamb,
Who once was wrapt in human frame;
They view within his bloody rays,
The object of eternal praife.

4 His fpirit fhews their fins forgiv'n,
And feals them for the heirs of heav'n;
And gives them patience here to wait,
'Till Jefus them to blifs tranflate.

5 He arms them for the evil day;
And while in heart with him they ftay,
He guides them with his mighty pow'r,
And brings them thro' the trying hour.

6 Then rest, my soul, upon thy Lord,
Ev'n Jesus Christ, the living word;
And then thy joy shall ne'er decay,
'Till it break out in endless day.

HYMN LXVI.

EPHESIANS II. 13.

1 OF him, who did salvation bring,
I cou'd for ever think and sing!
Arise, ye guilty, he'll forgive;
Arise, ye poor, he will relieve.

2 Eternal Lord, almighty king,
All heav'n doth with thy triumphs ring!
Thou conquer'st all, beneath, above,
Devils with force, and men with love!

3 Ask but his grace, and lo! 'tis giv'n,
Ask, and he turns your hell to heav'n;
Tho' sin and sorrow wound my soul,
Jesu, thy balm can make it whole.

4 Guide thou, O Lord, guide thou my course,
And draw me on with thy sweet force;
Still make me walk, still make me tend,
By thee my way, to God my end.

HYMN LXVII.

TO JESUS CHRIST.

1 O Thou, in whom the Gentiles trust,
　Thou only holy, only just;
　O tune our souls to praise thy name,
　Jesus! unchangeable, the same!

2 If angels, whilst to thee they sing,
　Wrap up their faces in their wing;
　How shall we sinful dust draw nigh,
　Thy great, and awful majesty?

3 Glory to thee, auspicious Lamb!
　Thou holy Lord, thou great I AM!
　With all our pow'r thy grace we bless,
　Our joy, our peace, our righteousness!

4 Live, ever glorious Jesus! live,
　Worthy all blessings to receive!
　Worthy on high enthron'd to sit,
　With ev'ry pow'r beneath thy feet!

5 Blessings for ever on the Lamb,
　Who bore the curse for sinful man;
　Let angels sound the sacred name,
　And ev'ry creature say AMEN.

HYMN LXVIII.

THE SAME.

1 HAIL thou once despised Jesus!
    Hail thou Galilean king!
Who didst suffer to release us,
    Who didst free salvation bring!
Hail thou universal Saviour,
    Who hast born our sin and shame,
By whose merits we find favour,
    Life is given thro' thy name!

2 Pascal Lamb by God appointed,
    All our sins were on thee laid!
By almighty love anointed,
    Thou hast full atonement made;
Ev'ry sin may be forgiv'n,
    Thro' the virtue of thy blood;
Open'd is the gate of heav'n,
    Peace is made 'twixt man and God.

3 Jesus hail! enthron'd in glory,
    There for ever to abide!
All the heav'nly hosts adore thee,
    Seated at thy father's side:
There for sinners thou art pleading,
    Spare them yet another year;—
Thou for saints art interceding,
    'Till in glory they appear.

4 Worship, honour, pow'r and blessing,
    Christ is worthy to receive—
Loudest praises without ceasing,
    Meet it is for us to give!
Help ye bright angelic spirits,
    Bring your sweetest, noblest lays,
Help to sing Christ Jesu's merits,
    Help to chaunt Immanuel's praise.

HYMN LXIX.

THE SAME.

1 COME, let us all unite to praise
    The Saviour of mankind,
Our thankful hearts in solemn lays,
    Be with our voices join'd.

2 But how shall dust his worth declare,
    When angels try in vain;
Their faces veil when they appear
    Before the son of man.

3 O Lord, we cannot silent be,
    By love we are constrain'd
To offer our best thanks to thee,—
    Our Saviour, and our friend!

4 Tho'

4 Tho' feeble are our best essays,
    Thy love will not despise;
Our grateful songs of humble praise,
    Our well-meant sacrifice.

5 Let ev'ry tongue thy goodness show,
    And spread abroad thy fame;
Let ev'ry heart with praise o'erflow,
    And bless thy sacred name!

6 Worship and honour, thanks and love,
    Be to our Jesus giv'n!
By men below—by hosts above—
    By all in earth and heav'n!

HYMN LXX.

REDEEMING LOVE.

1 NOW begin the heav'nly theme,
    Sing aloud in Jesu's name;
Ye, who Jesu's kindness prove,
Triumph in redeeming love.

2 Ye, who see the Father's grace,
    Beaming in the Saviour's face;
As to Canaan on ye move,
Praise and bless redeeming love.

3 Mourning souls dry up your tears,
  Banish all your guilty fears;
  See your guilt and curse remove,
  Cancell'd by redeeming love.

4 Ye, alas! who long have been
  Willing slaves of death and sin;
  Now from bliss no longer rove,
  Stop—and taste redeeming love.

5 Welcome all by sin opprest,
  Welcome all to Jesus Christ;
  Nothing brought him from above,
  Nothing but redeeming love.

6 He subdu'd th' infernal pow'rs,
  His tremendous foes and ours,
  From their cursed empire drove,
  Mighty in redeeming love.

7 Hither then your music bring,
  Strike aloud each joyful string;
  Mortals join the hosts above,
  Join to praise redeeming love.

HYMN

HYMN LXXI.

A PRAYER.

1 BE with me, Lord, where'er I go,
    Learn me what thou wou'd'ſt have me do;
    Suggeſt whate'er I think or ſay,
    Direct me in the narrow way.

2 Prevent me leſt I harbour pride,
    Leſt I in my own ſtrength confide;
    Shew me my weakneſs, let me ſee
    I have my pow'r, my all from thee.

3 Enrich me alway with thy love,
    My kind protection ever prove;
    Thy ſignet put upon my breaſt,
    And let thy ſpirit on me reſt.

4 Aſſiſt, and teach me how to pray,
    Incline my nature to obey;
    What thou abhorr'ſt, that let me flee,
    And only love what pleaſes thee.

5 O may I never do my will,
    But thine, and only thine fulfil;
    Let all my time, and all my ways
    Be ſpent, and ended to thy praiſe.

HYMN LXXII.

PSALM XCIII.

1 YE servants of God,
      Your master proclaim;
   And publish abroad
      His wonderful name:
   The name all-victorious
      Of Jesus **extol**;
   His kingdom is glorious,
      And rules over all.

2 God ruleth on high,
      Almighty to save;
   And still he is nigh,
      His presence we have:
   The great congregation
      His triumph shall sing,
   Ascribing salvation
      To Jesus our king.

3 Salvation to God,
      Who sits on the throne;
   Let all cry aloud,
      And honour the son:
   Our Jesus's praises
      The angel's proclaim,
   Fall down on their faces,
      And worship the Lamb.

4 Then

4   Then let us adore,
       And give him his right;
    All glory and pow'r,
       And wisdom and might:
    All honour and blessing,
       With angels above;
    And thanks never ceasing,
       And infinite love.

HYMN LXXIII.

TE DEUM.

1   HOW can we adore,
       Or worthily praise,
    Thy goodness and pow'r,
       Thou God of all grace!
    With honour and blessing
       Before thee we fall,
    Most gladly confessing
       Thee Father of all.

2   The heav'ns and earth,
       And water and air,
    To thee owe their birth,
       Subsist by thy care;
    While angels are singing
       Thy praises above,
    We mortals are bringing
       Our tribute of love.

3 Thou Saviour, art one
    With God the supreme,
His eternal son,
    And equal with him:
Invested with glory,
    On high dost thou sit,
While angels adore thee,
    And bow at thy feet.

4 How great was thy love!
    How wond'rous thy grace!
Thou cam'st from above
    To save a lost race;
And man to deliver,
    Of woman was born,
That ev'ry believer
    To God might return.

5 How soon will thy seat
    Of judgment appear!
Prepare us to meet,
    And welcome thee there!
Thy witnessing spirit
    In us shed abroad;
And bid us inherit
    The kingdom of God!

HYMN LXXIV.

UNDER TEMPTATION.

1 JESU, lover of my soul,
    Let me to thy bosom fly,
While the nearer waters roll,
    While the tempest still is high:
Hide me, O my Saviour, hide,
    'Till the storm of life is past;
Safe into the haven guide,
    O receive my soul at last!

2 Other refuge have I none,
    Hangs my helpless soul on thee,
Leave, ah! leave me not alone,
    Still support and comfort me:
All my trust on thee is stay'd,
    All my help from thee I bring;
Cover my defenceless head,
    With the shadow of thy wing.

3 Thou, O Christ, art all I want,
    More than all in thee I find;
Raise the fallen, chear the faint,
    Heal the sick and lead the blind:
Just and holy is thy name,
    I am all unrighteousness!
Vile, and full of sin I am,
    Thou art full of truth and grace.

4 Plenteous grace with thee is found,
   Grace to pardon all my sin:
Let the healing streams abound,
   Make, and keep me pure within:
Thou of life the fountain art,
   Freely let me take of thee;
Spring thou up within my heart,
   Rise to all eternity!

HYMN LXXV.

CHRIST OUR GREAT MELCHISEDEC.

1 THOU dear Redeemer, dying Lamb!
   We love to hear of thee;
No music's like thy charming name,
   Nor half so sweet can be!
O may we ever hear thy voice,
   In mercy to us speak!
And in our priest will we rejoice,
   Thou great Melchisedec!

2 Our Jesus shall be still our theme,
   While in this world we stay;
We'll sing our Jesu's lovely name,
   When all things else decay:
When we appear in yonder cloud,
   With all his favour'd throng;
Then will we sing more sweet, and loud,
   And Christ shall be our song.

HYMN LXXVI.

CHRIST OUR RIGHTEOUSNESS.

1 JESU, thy blood and righteousness,
   My beauty are, my glorious dress;
Midst flaming worlds in these array'd,
With joy shall I lift up my head.

2 When from the dust of death I rise,
To claim my mansion in the skies;
E'en then shall this be all my plea,
" Jesus hath LIV'D, hath DY'D for me."

3 Bold shall I stand in that great day,
For who ought to my charge shall lay?
Fully thro' thee absolv'd I am
From sin and fear, from guilt and shame.

4 Thus Abraham, the friend of God,
Thus all the armies bought with blood,
Saviour of sinners thee proclaim;
Sinners, of whom the chief I am.

5 This spotless robe the same appears,
When ruin'd nature sinks in years;
No age can change its glorious hue,
The grace of Christ is ever new.

6 O let the dead now hear thy voice,
   Now bid thy banish'd ones rejoice,
   Their beauty this, their glorious dress,
   Jesus, the Lord OUR RIGHTEOUSNESS.

HYMN LXXVII.

LONGING AFTER JESUS.

1 Dearest Jesus, come to me,
   And abide eternally;
   Worthy friend of sinners, come,
   Fill, and make my heart thine home.

2 Oftentimes for thee I sigh,
   Nothing else can give me joy;
   This is still my cry to thee,
   Dearest Jesus come to me.

3 Cou'd I clearly see above,
   What thy saints possess in love;
   All wou'd be but misery,
   Except Jesus was with me.

4 Son of God, my dearest Lord,
   All my crown, and my reward;
   Thou, who freely dy'd'st for me,
   Shalt alone my bridegroom be.

HYMN LXXVIII.

1 O Heavenly king,
    Look down from above;
Assist us to sing,
    Thy mercy and love:
So sweetly o'erflowing,
    So plenteous the store,
Thou still art bestowing,
    And giving us more.

2 O God of our life,
    We hallow thy name;
Our bus'ness and strife
    Is thee to proclaim:
Accept our thanksgiving
    For creating grace,
The living, the living
    Shall shew forth thy praise.

3 Our father and Lord,
    Almighty art thou;
Preserv'd by thy word,
    We worship thee now:
The bountiful donor
    Of all we enjoy;
Our tongues to thine honour,
    And lives we'll employ.

4   But O! above all
        Thy kindnefs we praife,
    From fin and from thrall
        Which faves a loft race;
    Thy fon thou haft giv'n
        A world to redeem,
    And bring us to heav'n,
        Whofe truft is in him.

5   Wherefore of thy love
        We fing and rejoice,
    With angels above
        We lift up our voice;
    Thy love each believer
        Shall gladly adore,
    For ever and ever,
        When time is no more.

HYMN LXXIX.

SALVATION.

1   Salvation! O the joyful found!
        What pleafure to our ears!
    A fov'reign balm for ev'ry wound,
        A cordial for our fears.

2   Salvation! let the eccho fly
        The fpacious earth around,
    While all the armies of the fky,
        Confpire to raife the found!

3 Salvation!

3 Salvation! O thou bleeding Lamb!
  To thee the praise belongs:
Salvation shall inspire our hearts,
  And dwell upon our tongues.

HYMN LXXX.

DESIRING PERSEVERANCE.

1 HAIL, Alpha and Omega, hail!
    Author of all our faith,
  The finisher of all our hopes,
    The truth, the life, the path.

2 Hail, first and last, the morning star,
    In whom we live and move;
  Increase our little spark of faith,
    And purify our love.

3 Let that belief, which Jesus taught,
    Be treasur'd in our breast;
  The evidence of unseen joys,
    The substance of our rest.

4 O let us go from strength to strength,
    From grace to greater grace,
  From one degree of faith to more,
    'Till we behold thy face.

HYMN LXXXI.

STRIVING TO PRAISE CHRIST.

1 LET us, the sheep by Jesus nam'd,
    Our shepherd's mercy bless;
Let us, whom Jesus hath redeem'd,
    Shew forth our thankfulness.

2 Not unto us, to thee alone,
    Be praise and glory giv'n;
Here shall thy praises be begun,
    But carry'd on in heav'n.

3 The hosts of spirits now with thee,
    Eternal anthems sing;
To imitate them here, lo! we
    Our hallelujahs bring.

4 Had we our tongues like them inspir'd,
    Like theirs our songs shou'd rise;
Like them we never shou'd be tir'd,
    But love the sacrifice.

5 'Till we this veil of flesh lay down,
    Accept our weaker lays;
And when, O Lord, we reach thy throne,
    We'll join in nobler praise.

HYMN LXXXII.

RESTING UNDER THE CROSS.

1 CHildren of Israel see what shade
    The cross does us afford;
It was for weary trav'lers made,
    We thank thee for it, Lord.

2 Here let us sit, and all prepare
    To sing his worthy fame;
Who to redeem us sojourn'd here,
    Christ Jesus is his name.

3 We sing thy suff'rings, wounds and blood,
    The virtue of thy pain;
We sing thy griefs, thou dying God,
    Thou Lamb for sinners slain.

4 We hail thee, thou by Jews revil'd,
    To thee we bow the knee;
Hail! very God, the promis'd child,
    The prophets sang of thee.

5 While others praise an unknown God,
    We each will sing of thee;
Jesus has wash'd me in his blood,
    And liv'd, and dy'd for me.

HYMN LXXXIII.

PRIVILEGES OF GOD's CHILDREN.

1 BLESSED are the sons of God,
   They are bought with Christ's own blood;
They are ransom'd from the grave,
Life eternal they shall have:
God did love them in his son,
Long before the world begun;
With them number'd may we be,
Here, and in eternity!

2 They the seal of this receive,
When on Jesus they beleive;
They are justify'd by grace,
They enjoy a solid peace:
All their sins are wash'd away,
They shall stand in God's great day,
With them number'd may we be,
Here, and in eternity!

3 They produce the fruits of grace,
In the works of righteousness;
They are harmless, meek and mild,
Holy, humble, undefil'd:
They are lights upon the earth,
Children of an heav'nly birth:
With them number'd may we be,
Here, and in eternity!

4 Born of God, they hate all fin,
God's pure feed remains within;
They have fellowfhip with God,
Thro' the mediator's blood:
One with God, with Jefus one,
Glory is in them begun;
With them number'd may we be,
Here, and in eternity!

5 Tho' they fuffer much on earth,
Strangers quite to this world's mirth;
Yet they have an inward joy,
Pleafures that can never cloy;
They alone are truly bleft,
Heirs of God, joint-heirs with Chrift;
With them number'd may we be,
Here, and in eternity!

HYMN LXXXIV.

1 O Come, thou wounded Lamb of God!
Come, wafh us in thy cleanfing blood;
Give us to know thy love, then pain
Is fweet, and life or death is gain.

2 Take our poor hearts, and let them be
For ever clos'd to all but thee;
Seal thou our breafts, and let us wear
That pledge of love for ever there.

3 How

3 How can it be thou heav'nly king,
That thou shou'd'st man to glory bring!
Make slaves the partners of thy throne,
And give them an immortal crown!

4 Ah, Lord! enlarge our scanty thought,
To know the wonders thou hast wrought;
Unloose our stamm'ring tongues to tell
Thy love immense, unsearchable.

5 First-born of many brethren, thou,
To thee both earth and heav'n must bow;
Help us to thee our all to give,
Thine may we die, thine may we live!

HYMN LXXXV.

1 O Jesu, Jesu, dearest Lord,
　　How wond'rous is thy love!
Thy patience, pity, tenderness,
　　Which I each moment prove!

2 O Lord, how faithless is my heart,
　　How apt to turn aside;
And wander in its own deceits,
　　Of reasoning and pride!

3 Yet dearest Saviour, love me still,
　　The poorest, and the worst;
For well I know where sin abounds,
　　Thy grace aboundeth most.

4 Yet let me not thy grace abuse,
    And sin because thou'rt good;
But let thy love fill me with shame,
    That I thy love withstood.

5 Saviour of sinners, now do this,
    Let me not turn away;
From thy dear cross, and bleeding wounds,
    But bind me there to stay!

6 On me, my king, exert thy pow'r,
    Make old things pass away;
Create all new, and draw me still,
    Still nearer ev'ry day.

7 I thank and praise thee, dearest Lord,
    For all that thou hast done,
O take me to thee as I am,
    For thy redeemed one!

HYMN LXXXVI.

1 Disciples of Christ,
    Ye friends of the Lamb;
Attend, and assist
    In singing his fame:
Eternal thanksgiving
    The faithful shou'd pay,
The living, the living,
    As we do this day.

2 A body of clay
  He humbly put on,
And then took away
  The sin we had done;
And in it endured
  The wrath to us due,
The curse we incurred,
  Our stripes and our woe.

3 Not only he dy'd,
  But also arose;
Laid weakness aside,
  And over his foes,
(Sin, death and the devil,)
  He triumphed o'er,
And every evil
  Dominion and pow'r.

4 O merciful Lamb,
  Who sits on the throne,
We bow at thy name,
  We count thee alone
Deserving our blessing,
  And blessing we'll give,
Without ever ceasing,
  So long as we live.

HYMN LXXXVII.

REJOICING IN HOPE.

1 MY Saviour, my almighty friend,
   When I begin to praise;
Where will the growing numbers end,
   The numbers of thy grace?

2 Thou art my everlasting trust,
   Thy goodness I adore!
Send down thy grace, O blessed Lord,
   That I may love thee more.

3 My feet shall travel all the length
   Of the celestial road;
And march with courage in thy strength,
   To see the Lord my God.

4 How will my lips rejoice to tell
   The victories of my king!
My soul redeem'd from sin and hell,
   Shall thy salvation sing.

5 My tongue shall all the day proclaim
   My Saviour, and my God;
His death has brought my foes to shame,
   And drown'd them in his blood.

6 Awake, awake my tuneful pow'rs,
  With this delightful song;
I'll entertain the darkest hours,
  Nor think the season long.

HYMN LXXXVIII.

TRUE FAITH.

1 O Love, thou bottomless abyss!
    My sins are swallow'd up in thee;
  Cover'd is my unrighteousness,
    From condemnation I am free;
  Whilst Jesu's blood thro' earth and skies,
  Mercy, free boundless mercy! cries.

2 With faith I plunge me in that sea;
    Here is my hope, my joy, my rest!
  Hither when hell assaults, I flee,
    I look into my Saviour's breast;
  Away sad doubts, and anxious fear,
  Mercy is all that's written there.

3 Tho' waves and storms go o'er my head,
    Tho' strength, and health, and friends be gone;
  Tho' joys be wither'd all and dead,
    Tho' ev'ry comfort be withdrawn:
  Stedfast on this my soul relies,
  Father thy mercy never dies!

4 Fixt

4 Fixt on this ground wou'd I remain,
    Tho' my heart fail, and flesh decay;
This anchor shall my soul sustain,
    When earth's foundations melt away:
Mercy's full pow'r I then shall prove,
Lov'd with an everlasting love.

HYMN LXXXIX.

FOR THE SPIRIT OF ADOPTION.

1 FATHER, (if thou my father art)
    Send forth the Spirit of thy son;
Breathe him into my panting heart,
    And make me know as I am known;
Make me thy conscious child, that I
May Father, Abba, Father, cry!

2 O that the comforter wou'd come,
    Nor visit as a transient guest;
But fix in me his constant home,
    And keep possession of my breast;
And make my soul his lov'd abode,
The temple of in-dwelling God!

3 Come, holy Ghost, my soul inspire,
    Attest that I am born again;
Come and baptize me, Lord, with fire,
    Nor let thy former gifts be vain:
O grant the sense of sin forgiv'n,
O grant the earnest of my heav'n.

4 O give th' indisputable seal,
   That ascertains the kingdom mine!
That pow'rful stamp I long to feel,
   The signature of love divine:
O shed it in my heart abroad,
Fulness of love, of heav'n, of God!

HYMN XC.

A PRAYER FOR GRACE.

1 AH! Lord, how faithless is my heart,
   How very apt from thee to stray!
Just like a broken bow I start,
   And nature strives to bear the sway:
Was ever one so vile, so blest!
So foul, yet by the Lamb caress'd!

2 Forbid, O Lord, each vain desire,
   And bind my passions to thy cross;
Quench all the sparks of nature's fire,
   And bid me count my gain but loss:
Lord Jesus, tear each idol down,
And 'stablish in my heart thy throne.

3 O let thy grace wipe off my tears,
   And speak the tempest to a calm;
O warm my heart, and charm my fears,
   Be thou a never failing balm;
The maladies of sin remove,
And fill my soul with heav'nly love.

4 Henceforth I'd serve thee, if thou'lt please
   To gird me with an heav'nly pow'r;
 I'd sing the glories of thy grace
   'Till all my pilgrimage be o'er:
 With hallow'd fire inspire my tongue,
 And love shall be my endless song.

HYMN XCI.

CREATION AND REDEMPTION.

1 GIVE to our God immortal praise!
   Mercy and truth are all his ways;
 Wonders of grace to God belong,
 Repeat his mercies in your song.

2 Give to the Lord of Lords renown,
 The king of kings with glory crown;
 His mercies ever shall endure,
 When lords and kings are known no more.

3 He built the earth, he spread the sky,
 And fixt the starry lights on high:
 Wonders of grace to God belong,
 Repeat his mercies in your song.

4 He fills the sun with morning light,
 He bids the moon direct the night:
 His mercies ever shall endure,
 When suns and moons shall shine no more.

5 He sent his son with pow'r to save
From guilt, and darkness, and the grave,
Wonders of grace to God belong;
Repeat his mercies in your song.

6 Thro' this vain world he guides our feet,
And leads us to his heav'nly seat;
His mercies ever shall endure,
When this vain world shall be no more.

HYMN XCII.

AN HAPPY MOMENT.

1 SAviour, I do feel thy merit,
 Sprinkled with redeeming blood;
And my weary, troubled spirit
 Now finds rest in thee, my God:
I am safe, and I am happy,
 Whilst in thy dear arms I lie;
Sin and satan cannot hurt me,
 Whilst the Saviour is so nigh.

2 Now I'll sing of Jesu's merit,
 Tell the world of his dear name;
That if any want his spirit,
 He is still the very same:
He that asketh, soon receiveth,
 He that seeks is sure to find;
Come, for whosoe'er believeth,
 He will never cast behind.

3 Now our advocate is pleading
  With his Father, and our God;
Now for us he's interceding,
  As the purchase of his blood:
Now methinks I hear him praying,
  Father, save them, I have dy'd;
And the Father, answers, saying,
  They are freely justify'd.

HYMN XCIII.

1 THroughout the Saviour's life we trace,
    Nothing, but shame and deep disgrace;
      No period else is seen;
  'Till he a spotless victim fell,
  Tasting in soul a painful hell,
      Caus'd by the creature's sin.

2 On the cold ground methinks I see
  My Jesus kneel, and pray for me;
      For this I him adore:
  Seiz'd with a chilly sweat throughout,
  Blood-drops did force their passage out,
      Thro' ev'ry open'd pore.

3 A pricking thorn his temples bore,
  His back with lashes all was tore,
      'Till one the bones might see;
  Mocking they push'd him here and there,
  Marking his way with blood and tear,
      Press'd by the heavy tree.

4. Thus

4 Thus up the hill he painful came,
  Round him they mock, and make their game,
    At length his cross they rear;
  And can you see the mighty God
  Cry out beneath sin's heavy load,
    Without one thankful tear?

5 Thus veiled in humanity,
  He dies in anguish on the tree;
    What tongue his griefs can tell?
  The shudd'ring rocks their heads recline,
  The mourning sun refus'd to shine,
    When the creator fell.

6 Shout, brethren, shout in songs divine;
  He drank the gall to give us wine,
    To quench our parching thirst:
  Seraphs advance your voices higher;
  Bride of the Lamb unite the choir,
    And laud thy precious Christ.

HYMN XCIV.

1 O Thou tender loving Jesus,
    Now thy saving grace impart;
  From the world and satan save us,
    Save us from our evil heart:
  Throw thine arms in mercy open,
    Bid, O bid us Jesus, come;
  Let our flinty hearts be broken,
    Falling on the corner-stone.

2 Here for ever let us center
    Steady, tho' assail'd by sin;
Forward may we stoutly venture,
    'Till eternal life we win:
Banish ev'ry reas'ning scruple,
    Scatter ev'ry gathering cloud;
Our poor hearts, O Jesus, sprinkle,
    Sprinkle with thy precious blood.

3 When our chearing feelings sicken,
    And a veil our souls o'erspreads;
Then with grace our spirits quicken,
    And raise up our drooping heads;
When our foolish hearts would wander
    From the source of real joy;
Call us back, but not in anger,
    Left thy fury us destroy.

4 Arm us from thy heav'nly store-house,
    Still display thy banner high,
March victorious on before us,
    Make the world and satan fly:
When thy messenger arraigns us,
    To close up our weary eyes,
In that needy hour sustain us,
    'Till we grasp the heav'nly prize.

HYMN

HYMN XCV.

ADORING CHRIST.

1 O For a thousand tongues to sing,
    My dear Redeemer's praise!
The glories of my God and king,
    The triumphs of his grace.

2 Jesus, the name that charms our fears,
    That bids our sorrows cease;
'Tis music in the sinner's ears,
    'Tis life, and health, and peace.

3 He breaks the pow'r of cancel'd sin,
    He sets the pris'ners free;
His blood can make the foulest clean,
    His blood avail'd for me.

4 He speaks, and list'ning to his voice,
    New life the dead receive;
The mournful, broken hearts rejoice,
    The humble poor believe.

5 Hear him, ye deaf; his praise, ye dumb,
    Your loosen'd tongues employ;
Ye blind, behold your Saviour come,
    And **leap,** ye lame, for joy.

HYMN XCVI.

CONFIDENCE.

1 With all my pow'rs of heart and tongue,
   I'll praise my maker in my song:
Angels shall hear the notes I raise,
Approve the song, and join the praise.

2 I'll sing thy truth and mercy, Lord,
I'll sing the wonders of thy word;
Not all thy works, and names below,
So much thy pow'r and glory shew.

3 To God I cry'd when trouble rose,
He heard me, and subdu'd my foes;
He did my rising fears controul,
And strength diffus'd thro' all my soul.

4 Amidst a thousand snares I stand
Upheld, and guarded by thy hand;
Thy words my fainting soul revive,
And keep my dying faith alive.

5 Grace will compleat what grace begins,
To save from sorrows, or from sins;
The work that wisdom undertakes,
Eternal mercy ne'er forsakes.

HYMN XCVII.

JOY IN CHRIST.

1 MY dear Redeemer, dying Lord,
    I love to hear of thee;
Thy name doth grace and life afford
    To sinful souls, like me.

2 Thy precious name so warms my heart,
    And sets my soul on flame;
I wou'd not, Lord, from thee depart,
    But always love thy name.

3 I live, because my Saviour dy'd,
    Above the pow'r of sin;
Hereby I'm freely justify'd,
    Because he 'rose again.

4 I'm lost in wonder when I see
    His grievous bitter smart;
And how he liv'd and dy'd for me;
    This breaks my stony heart.

5 O! then I blush, and nothing say,
    But silently fall down,
Like Sheba's queen, and faint away
    Before king Solomon.

6 Chrift lives in me, and I in him,
    The happy life of faith;
E'er long he will deftroy my fin,
    And quite abolifh death.

HYMN XCVIII.

THE SAME.

1 O Dear Redeemer, who alone
    Canft give me eafe in pain;
Whofe blood did once for fin atone,
    And pardon for me gain.

2 I once was wholly dead in fin,
    And ignorant of thee;
And walk'd contentedly therein,
    Nor knew thy love to me.

3 But thine all-feeing eye then view'd,
    And mark'd my ev'ry way,
And ftill in tender love purfu'd
    Me, who from thee did ftray.

4 Thy name is now thro' grace become
    More precious to my foul,
Than fweeteft fmell of rich perfume,
    Or Aaron's precious oil.

5 Without thy favour tho' I live,
  Life but a burden is;
Nought else can satisfaction give,
  Experience shews me this.

6 My faithless heart, O Saviour dear,
  Correct with gentle hand;
In every danger be thou near,
  Alone I cannot stand.

HYMN XCIX.

UNIVERSAL PRAISE.

1 THE glories of my maker, God,
    My joyful voice shall sing,
  And call the nation to adore
    Their former and their king.

2 'Twas his right-hand that shap'd our clay,
    And wrought this human frame;
  But from his own immediate breath
    Our nobler spirits came.

3 We bring our mortal pow'rs to God,
    And worship with our tongues;
  We claim some kindred with the skies,
    And join th' angelic songs.

4 Let grov'ling beasts of ev'ry shape,
   And fowls of ev'ry wing,
 And rocks, and trees, and fires, and seas,
   Their various tribute bring.

5 Ye planets to his honour shine,
   And wheels of nature roll;
 Praise him in your unweary'd course,
   Around the steady pole.

6 The brightness of our maker's name
   The wide creation fills,
 And his unbounded grandeur flies
   Beyond the heav'nly hills.

HYMN C.

A DIVINE RAPTURE.

1 FROM thee, my God, my joys shall rise,
   And run eternal rounds,
 Beyond the limits of the skies,
   And all created bounds.

2 The holy triumphs of my soul
   Shall death itself out-brave,
 Leave dull mortality behind,
   And fly beyond the grave.

3 There,

3 There, where my blessed Jesus reigns,
    In heav'n's unmeasur'd space
I'll spend a long eternity,
    In pleasure and in praise.

4 Millions of years my wond'ring eyes
    Shall o'er thy beauties rove,
And endless ages I'll adore
    The glories of thy love.

5 Sweet Jesus, ev'ry smile of thine
    Shall fresh endearments bring,
And thousand tastes of new delight,
    From all thy graces spring.

6 Haste, my beloved, fetch my soul
    Up to thy bless'd abode;
Fly, for my spirit longs to see
    My Saviour, and my God.

HYMN CI.

GOD ALL IN ALL.

1 MY God, my life, my love,
    To thee, to thee, I call;
I cannot live if thou remove,
    For thou art all in all.

2 Thy shining grace can chear
  This dungeon where I dwell;
'Tis paradise when thou art here,
  If thou depart 'tis hell.

3 The smilings of thy face,
  How lovely, Lord, they are!
'Tis heav'n to rest in thine embrace,
  And no where else but there.

4 To thee, and thee alone
  The angels owe their bliss;
They sit around thy gracious throne,
  And dwell where Jesus is.

5 Nor earth, nor all the sky,
  Can one delight afford;
No not one drop of real joy,
  Without thy presence, Lord.

6 Be thou the sea of love,
  Where all my pleasures roll;
The circle where my passions move,
  And centre of my soul.

7 To thee my spirits fly,
  With fulness of desire;
Yet very far from thee I lie,
  Dear Jesus, raise me higher.

HYMN

HYMN CII.

PRAISE TO THE REDEEMER.

1 Plung'd in a gulph of dark despair,
    We wretched sinners lay,
Without one chearing beam of hope,
    Or spark of glimm'ring day.

2 With pitying eyes the prince of grace
    Beheld our helpless grief;
He saw, and (O amazing love!)
    He ran to our relief.

3 Down from the shining seats above,
    With joyful haste he fled;
Enter'd the grave in mortal flesh,
    And dwelt among the dead.

4 Oh! for this love, let rocks and hills
    Their lasting silence break;
And all harmonious human tongues
    The Saviour's praises speak.

5 Angels assist our mighty joys,
    Strike all your harps of gold;
But when you raise your highest notes,
    His love can ne'er be told.

HYMN CIII.

PROTECTION FROM ENEMIES.

1 ARISE my soul, my joyful pow'rs,
    And triumph in thy God;
Awake my voice, and loud proclaim
    His glorious grace abroad.

2 He rais'd me from the deeps of sin,
    The gates of gaping hell;
And fix'd my standing more secure
    Than 'twas before I fell.

3 The arms of everlasting love
    Beneath my soul he plac'd;
And on the rock of ages set
    My slippery footsteps fast.

4 The city of my blest abode
    Is wall'd around with grace;
Salvation for a bulwark stands,
    To shield the sacred place.

5 Satan may vent his sharpest spite,
    And all his legions roar;
Almighty mercy guards my life,
    And bounds his raging pow'r.

6 Arise my soul, awake my voice,
   And songs of praises sing;
Loud hallelujahs shall address
   My Saviour, and my king.

HYMN CIV.

GOD OUR ONLY HAPPINESS.

1 MY God, my portion, and my love,
   My everlasting all;
I've none but thee in heav'n above,
   Or on this earthly ball.

2 What empty things are all the skies,
   And this inferior clod!
There's nothing here deserves my joys,
   There's nothing like my God.

3 In vain the bright, the burning sun,
   Scatters his feeble light;
'Tis thy sweet beams create my noon,
   If thou withdraw 'tis night.

4 And whilst upon my restless bed,
   Amidst the shades I roll;
If my Redeemer shews his head,
   'Tis morning with my soul.

5 To thee we owe our wealth and friends,
    And health, and safe abode;
  We praise thy name for all these things,
    But they are not my God.

6 How vain a toy is glitt'ring wealth,
    If once compar'd to thee?
  And what's my safety, or my health,
    Or all my friends to me?

7 Were I possessor of the earth,
    And call'd the stars my own;
  Without my Jesus, and thyself,
    I were a wretch undone.

7 Let other stretch their arms like seas,
    And grasp in all the shore;
  Grant me the visits of thy face,
    And I desire no more.

HYMN CV.

FAITH's CLAIM.

1   ALL ye that pass by,
      To Jesus draw nigh,
To you is it nothing that Jesus shou'd die?
    Your ransom and peace,
    Your surety he is,
Come see if there ever was sorrow like his.

2   For what you have done
      His blood muſt atone;
The father hath puniſh'd for you his dear ſon:
        He anſwer'd for all,
        O come at his call,
And low at his croſs with aſtoniſhment fall.

3   For you and for me
      He pray'd on the tree;
The prayer is accepted, the ſinner is free;
        That ſinner am I,
        Who on Jeſus rely,
And come for the pardon God cannot deny.

4   My pardon I claim,
      For a ſinner I am,
A ſinner believing in Jeſus's name:
        He purchas'd the grace,
        Which now I embrace,
O father thou know'ſt he hath dy'd in my place.

5   His death is my plea,
      My advocate fee,
And hear the blood ſpeak, that hath anſwer'd for me;
        Acquitted I was,
        When he bled on the croſs,
And by loſing his life he hath carry'd my cauſe.

L   H Y M N

HYMN CVI.

THE WAY TO CANAAN.

1 JESUS my all, to heav'n is gone,
   He whom I fix my hopes upon;
   His track I see, and I'll pursue
   The narrow way 'till him I view.

2 The way the holy prophets went,
   The road that leads from banishment;
   The king's highway of holiness
   I'll go, for all his paths are peace.

3 This is the way I long have sought,
   And mourn'd because I found it not;
   My grief a burden long has been,
   Because I could not cease from sin.

4 The more I strove against its pow'r,
   I sinn'd, and stumbl'd but the more;
   'Till late I heard my Saviour say,
   Come hither, soul, "I AM THE WAY."

5 Lo! glad I come, and thou bless'd Lamb
   Shalt take me to thee as I am;
   Nothing but sin I thee can give,
   Nothing but love shall I receive.

6 Then

6 Then will I tell to sinners round,
   What a dear Saviour I have found;
   I'll point to thy redeeming blood,
   And say, "Behold THE WAY TO GOD."

HYMN CVII.

PRAISE YE THE LORD.

1 Lord and God of heav'nly pow'rs, Hallelujah
     Theirs, and O benignly ours; Hallelujah
   Glorious king, let earth proclaim, Hallelujah
   Worms attempt to sing thy name. Hallelujah

2 Bow thine ear, in mercy bow,   Hallelujah
   Hear, the world's atonement thou; Hallelujah
   Jesus, in thy name we pray,   Hallelujah
   Take, O take our sins away.   Hallelujah

3 Thee to laud in songs divine,   Hallelujah
   Angels and archangels join;   Hallelujah
   We with them our voices raise,   Hallelujah
   Echoing thine eternal praise.   Hallelujah

4 Holy, holy, holy Lord!   Hallelujah
   Live, by heav'n and earth ador'd: Hallelujah
   Full of thee they ever cry,   Hallelujah
   "Glory be to God on high."   Hallelujah

HYMN CVIII.

1 O Jesus, everlasting God,
   Who once for sinners shed'st thy blood
      Upon mount Calvary;
   And finish'd there redemption's toil,
   And mad'st lost man thy happy spoil:
      All glory be to thee.

2 Fain would I think upon thy pain,
   And find therein my life and gain,
      And fix my heart and mind,
   Upon thy wounds and dying love;
   Nor from the same my heart remove,
      'Till all thy heav'n I find.

3 Content and glad I'll ever be
   To have salvation, Lord, from thee,
      E'en as a sinner poor;
   I nothing have, I nothing am;
   My treasure's in the bleeding Lamb,
      Both now and evermore.

4 The more thro' grace myself I know,
   The more content I am to bow,
      And sink beneath thy cross:
   And live by faith upon thy blood,
   Waiting on thee for ev'ry good,
      And count my gain but loss.

HYMN CIX.

1 MY Lord, I'm fill'd with wonder,
    To find thee still so kind;
When I intensely ponder
    The coldness of my mind:
My numberless omissions,
    My negligence in pray'r;
My manifold commissions,
    And wand'rings here and there.

2 How many vile affections
    Surviving vex my heart;
How strong are those corruptions
    Which warring give me smart?
The world, the flesh, and devil,
    Strive to usurp the sway;
Still tempting me to evil,
    To lead my soul astray.

3 Instead of loud thanksgiving,
    Wherein I ought t'abound,
I'm subject to complaining,
    When trials me surround:
My want of resignation,
    Disorders me within;
Gives birth unto temptation,
    To unbelief and sin.

4 But soon I am ashamed
   Such thoughts to entertain;
Why should my Lord be blamed
   When in the fault I am?
'Tis thine to be forgiving
   The penetential race;
And mine to be receiving
   The bounties of thy grace.

HYMN CX.

HUMAN WEAKNESS OWNED.

1 MY Lord, how great's the favour!
   That I a sinner poor,
Can thro' thy blood's sweet favour
   Approach thy mercy's door:
And find an open passage
   Unto the throne of grace;
There wait the welcome message,
   That bids me go in peace.

2 Lord, I'm an helpless creature,
   Full of the deepest need,
Throughout defil'd by nature,
   Stupid, and inly dead:
My strength is perfect weakness,
   And all I have is sin;
My heart is all uncleanness,
   A den of theives within.

3 In this forlorn condition,
　　Who shall afford me aid?
Where shall I meet compassion
　　But in the church's head?
Jesus, thou art all pity,
　　O take me to thine arms,
And exercise thy mercy,
　　To save me from all harms.

4 I'll never cease repeating
　　My numberless complaints;
But ever be entreating
　　The glorious king of saints,
'Till I attain the image
　　Of him I inly love;
And pay my grateful homage
　　With all the saints above.

5 Then I, with all in glory,
　　Will thankfully relate
Th' amazing, pleasing story
　　Of Jesu's love so great;
In this blest contemplation
　　I ever shall be well;
And prove such consolation,
　　As none below can tell.

HYMN

HYMN CXI.

EXULTING IN CHRIST.

1 THE despised Nazarene,
    Who is chief in my esteem;
Mark'd with scourges, nails and spear,
Hung an ensign in the air.

2 None among the sons of men,
None among the heav'nly train,
Can with my belov'd compare,
Who to me is ever dear.

3 Had I Gabriel's heav'nly tongue,
He shou'd ever be my song;
Object of my present bliss,
Subject of my future praise.

4 Ravish'd I'm beyond degree,
While I view him on the tree;
All his wounds and bruises are
To my soul exceeding fair.

5 Other lovers I despise;
Mine is gone beyond the skies:
Earthly things are far too mean
To divert me from the Lamb.

6 How my Lord shall I set forth
All thy dignity and worth!
Human words cannot express
Half thy love, or half thy peace.

7 From thy fulness me supply
Of thy grace to testify,
Let my fellow creatures prove
What is tasted in thy love.

8 Soul and body sink with shame,
While I thee, my Saviour, name;
Soul and body Lord set free
In the gospel-liberty.

HYMN CXII.

HEBREWS VI. 17—19.

1 HOW oft have sin and satan strove
To rend my soul from thee, my God?
But everlasting is thy love,
And Jesus seals it with his blood.

2 Amidst temptations sharp and long,
My soul to this dear refuge flies;
Hope, is my anchor firm and strong,
While tempests blow, and billows rise.

3. The

3 The gospel bears my spirits up;
   A faithful and unchanging God
Lays the foundation for my hope,
   In oaths, and promises, and blood.

HYMN CXIII.

LOVE.

1 O Love divine, how sweet thou art!
   When shall we find our longing heart
  All taken up by thee?
Oh! may we pant and thirst to prove,
The greatness of redeeming love,
   The love of Christ so free.

2 God only knows the love of God,
   O that it now were shed abroad
    In each poor longing heart!
For love I'd sigh, for love I'd pine,
This only portion, Lord, be mine,
   Be mine this better part.

3 O that we cou'd for ever sit
   With Mary, at the master's feet,
    Be this our happy choice!
Our only care, delight, and bliss,
Our joy, our heav'n on earth be this,
   To hear the bridegroom's voice.

4 Thy

4 Thy only love may we require,
  Nothing on earth beneath desire,
    Nothing in heaven above:
  Let earth and all its trifles go,
  Give us, O Lord! thy love to know,
    Give us thy precious love!

HYMN CXIV.

1 JOHN IV. 16. LATTER PART.

1 LOVE divine, all love excelling,
    Joy of heav'n to earth come down!
  Fix in us thine humble dwelling,
    All thy faithful mercies crown:
  Jesus! thou art all compassion,
  Pure, unbounded love thou art;
  Visit us with thy salvation,
  Enter ev'ry trembling heart!

2 Breathe, O breathe thy loving spirit,
    Into ev'ry troubl'd breast!
  Let us all in thee inherit,
    Let us find thy promis'd rest:
  Take away the pow'r of sinning,
  Alpha and Omega be,
  End of faith, as its beginning,
  Set our hearts at liberty.

3 Come, almighty to deliver,
  Let us all thy life receive!
  Suddenly return, and never,
  Never more thy temples leave!
  Thee we wou'd be always blessing,
  Serve thee as thine hosts above,
  Pray, and praise thee without ceasing,
  Glory in thy precious love.

4 Finish then thy new creation,
  Pure, unspotted may we be,
  Let us see thy great salvation,
  Perfectly restor'd by thee!
  Chang'd from glory into glory,
  'Till in heav'n we take our place,
  'Till we cast our crowns before thee,
  Lost in wonder, love, and praise.

HYMN CXV.

THE GOODNESS OF GOD.

1 SWEET is the mem'ry of thy grace,
    My God, my heav'nly king!
  Sweet is the mem'ry of thy grace;
  Let age to age thy righteousness
    In sounds of glory sing,
  Sweet is the mem'ry of thy grace.

2 God

2 God reigns on high, but not confines
    His goodneſs to the ſkies,
Sweet is the mem'ry of thy grace;
Thro' the whole earth his goodneſs ſhines,
    And ev'ry want ſupplies;
Sweet is the mem'ry of thy grace.

3 With longing eyes thy creatures wait
    On thee for daily food;
Sweet is the mem'ry of thy grace;
Thy lib'ral hand provides them meat,
    And fills their mouths with good;
Sweet is the mem'ry of thy grace.

4 How kind are thy compaſſions, Lord!
    How ſlow thine anger moves!
Sweet is the mem'ry of thy grace:
But ſoon he ſends his pard'ning word
    To chear the ſoul he loves;
Sweet is the mem'ry of thy grace.

5 Creatures, with all their endleſs race,
    Thy pow'r and praiſe proclaim:
Sweet is the mem'ry of thy grace:
May we, who taſte thy richer grace,
    Delight to bleſs thy name!
Sweet is the mem'ry of thy grace.

HYMN

HYMN CXVI.

THANSGIVING.

1 MEET and right it is to sing
 Glory to our God and king;
 Meet in ev'ry time and place,
 To rehearse his solemn praise.

2 Join, ye saints, the song around,
 Angels, help the solemn sound;
 Publish thro' the world abroad
 Glory to th' eternal God.

3 Praises here to thee we give,
 Gracious thou our thanks receive;
 Holy father, sov'reign Lord,
 Ev'ry where be thou ador'd!

4 Tho' th' injurious world exclaim,
 Sing we still in Jesu's name;
 Saviour thee we ever bless,
 Thee, our Lord and God confess.

HYMN CXVII.

HEAVENLY JOY ON EARTH.

1 COME ye that love the Lord,
    And let your joys be known;
Join in a song with sweet accord,
    While ye surround the throne.

2 The sorrows of the mind
    Be banish'd from the place;
Religion never was design'd
    To make our pleasures less.

3 Let those refuse to sing,
    Who never knew our God;
But children of the heav'nly king
    Will speak their joys abroad.

4 The men of grace have found
    Glory begun below;
Celestial fruits on earthly ground,
    From faith and hope may grow.

5 The hill of Zion yields
    A thousand sacred sweets,
Before we reach the heav'nly fields,
    Or walk the golden streets.

6 Then let our songs abound,
And ev'ry tear be dry;
We're marching thro' Immanuel's ground,
To fairer worlds on high.

HYMN CXVIII.

OFFICES OF CHRIST.

1 JOIN all the glorious names,
Of wisdom, love, and pow'r,
That mortals ever knew,
That angels ever bore:
All are too mean
To speak his worth,
Too mean to set
Our Saviour forth.

2 But O! what gentle terms,
What condescending ways,
Doth our Redeemer use
To teach his heav'nly grace!
My soul, with joy,
And wonder, see
What forms of love
He bears for thee.

3 Great

3 Great prophet of our God,
Our tongues wou'd blefs thy name!
By thee the joyful news
Of our falvation came:
  The joyful news
    Of fins forgiv'n,
  Of hell fubdu'd,
    And peace with heav'n.

4 Jefus, our great high-prieft,
Offer'd his blood, and dy'd;
Thou guilty finner feek
No facrifice befide:
  His pow'rful blood
    Did once atone,
  And now it pleads
    Before the throne.

5 Thou dear almighty Lord!
Our conqu'ror, and our king!
Thy fcepter, and thy fword,
Thy reigning grace we fing:
  Thine is the pow'r;
    O may we fit,
  In willing bonds,
    Beneath thy feet!

HYMN CXIX.

THE SAME.

1 ARray'd in mortal flesh,
    Lo the great angel stands!
And holds the promises
    And pardons in his hands:
      Commission'd from
        His father's throne,
      To make his grace
        To mortals known.

2 Be thou our counsellor,
    Our pattern, and our guide!
And thro' this desart land,
    Still keep us near thy side!
      O let our feet
        Ne'er run astray,
      Nor rove, nor seek
        The crooked way!

3 We'd hear our shepherd's voice,
    Whose watchful eye doth keep
Poor wand'ring souls among
    The thousands of his sheep:
      He feeds his flock,
        He calls their names,
      His bosom bears
        The tender lambs.

4 To this dear surety's hands,
    My soul, commend thy cause;
He answers, and fulfils
    His father's broken laws:
      Believing souls
        Now free are set;
      For Christ hath paid
        Their dreadful debt.

5 Then let our souls arise,
    And tread the tempter down;
Our captain leads us forth
    To conquest and a crown:
      March on! nor fear
        To win the day,
      Tho' death and hell
        Obstruct the way.

HYMN CXX.

1 LORD avenge thy tempted saints,
    For thou canst supply our wants;
Satan and a sinful heart,
Cause us many hours of smart:
We sail on a troubled sea,
Harrass'd by the enemy;
Foes without, and foes within,
Tempting daily unto sin.

2 Satan uses all his craft,
  On the right hand, and the left;
  World and flesh, and hell combine,
  Jesus, send thy help divine:
  God his little remnant tries,
  Salts with fire each sacrifice;
  But tho' tempests rise afresh—
  Christ is in the burning bush.

3 Lord, thy dealings we admire,
  Thou'lt us save, yet as by fire;
  Purge the dross, the gold refine,
  Stamp the same for current coin:
  Jesu, we can find no rest,
  But when leaning on thy breast;
  Onward then we sweetly move,
  When we suck the breasts of love.

4 We shall surely find at length
  Weakness perfected in strength;
  Tho' we're tost with doubts and fears,
  Thou wilt wipe away our tears:
  Lord bring on the joyful day,
  Make our sorrows flee away;
  Gather all thy saints in one,
  Thee to praise around the throne.

HYMN

HYMN CXXI.

1 GLORY be to God on high, Hallelujah
   God, whose glory fills the sky, Hallelujah
   Peace on earth to man forgiv'n, Hallelujah
   Man the well-belov'd of heav'n. Hallelujah

2 Sov'reign father, heav'nly king, Hallelujah
   Thee we now presume to sing, Hallelujah
   Glad thine attributes confess, Hallelujah
   Glorious all, and numberless. Hallelujah

3 Hail by all thy works ador'd, Hallelujah
   Hail the everlasting Lord; Hallelujah
   Thee with thankful hearts we prove Hallelujah
   Lord of pow'r, and God of love! Hallelujah

HYMN CXXII.

THE SINNER CONVERTED.

1 WHEN with my mind devoutly prest,
    Dear Saviour, my revolving breast
   Wou'd past offences trace;
   Trembling I make the black review,
   Yet pleas'd behold, admiring too,
    The **pow'r** of changing grace.

2 This tongue with blasphemies defil'd,
  These feet to erring paths beguil'd,
    In heav'nly league agree;
  Who cou'd believe such lips cou'd praise,
  Or think my dark and winding ways
    Shou'd ever lead to thee?

3 These eyes, that once abus'd their sight,
  Now lift to thee their watry light,
    And weep a silent flood;
  These hands ascend in ceaseless pray'r;
  O wash away the stains they wear,
    In pure redeeming blood!

4 These ears, that pleas'd cou'd entertain
  The midnight oath, the lustful strain,
    When round the festal board;
  Now deaf to all th'inchanting noise,
  Avoid the throng, detest the joys,
    And press to hear thy word.

5 Thus art thou serv'd in ev'ry part;
  And now thou dost transform my heart,
    That drossy thing refine:
  Now grace doth nature's strength controul,
  And a new creature—body—soul—
    Are, Lord, for ever thine.

HYMN

HYMN CXXIII.

THE SAME.

1 OFT I reflect upon the grace,
    With tears of thankfulness;
Which call'd me from my native place,
    The world's wide wilderness.

2 My precious time I vainly spent,
    Subject to nature's sway;
My corrupt carnal will was bent,
    Its motions to obey.

3 Thick darkness overspread my mind,
    I stumbled in the night;
All my affections were inclin'd
    To creaturely delight.

4 God saw me in this wretched case,
    A slave to base desire;
And by an act of special grace,
    The brand pluck'd from the fire.

5 My heart throughout defil'd by sin,
    The holy Ghost renew'd;
And each unruly ill within
    Thro' conqu'ring grace subdu'd.

6 Satan's dominion he destroy'd,
    And spoke me into peace;
My soul a perfect calm enjoy'd,
    And solac'd in the bliss.

7 Still may a sense of mercies past,
    Stir up my soul to praise;
And whet my appetite to taste
    Thy larger draughts of grace.

HYMN CXXIV.

THE BELIEVER's HOPE.

1 HE is a God of sov'reign love,
    That promis'd heav'n to me;
And taught my thoughts to soar above,
    Where happy spirits be.

2 Prepare me, Lord, for thy right hand,
    Then come the joyful day!
Come death, and some celestial band,
    To bear my soul away.

3 Then, my beloved, take my soul,
    Up to thy blest abode;
That face to face I may behold
    My Saviour, and my God.

HYMN CXXV.

PSALM CXIX. VERSE CLVIII.

1 ARISE, my tend'rest thoughts, arise,
  To torrents melt my streaming eyes!
  And thou, my heart, with anguish feel
  Those evils, which thou canst not heal!

2 See human nature sunk in shame!
  See scandals pour'd on Jesu's name!
  The Father wounded thro' the son!
  The world abus'd, the soul undone!

3 See the short course of vain delight
  Closing in everlasting night!
  In flames, that no abatement know,
  The briny tears for ever flow.

4 My God, I feel the mournful scene;
  My bowels yearn o'er dying men;
  And fain my pity wou'd reclaim,
  And snatch the firebrands from the flame!

5 But feeble my compassion proves,
  And can but weep where most it loves;
  Thine own all-saving arm employ,
  And turn those drops of grief to joy.

HYMN CXXVI.

THE CHRISTIAN's CHARGE.

1   A Charge to keep I have,
       A God to glorify;
    A never-dying soul to save,
       And fit it for the sky.

2   To serve the present age,
       My calling to fulfill;
    O may it all my pow'rs engage,
       To do my master's will!

3   Arm me with jealous care,
       As in thy sight to live;
    And O! thy servant, Lord prepare,
       A good account to give!

4   Help me to watch and pray,
       And on thyself rely;
    And let me ne'er my trust betray,
       Lest I for ever die.

HYMN CXXVII.

FAITH IN CHRIST OUR SACRIFICE.

1 NOT all the blood of beasts,
  On Jewish altars slain;
Cou'd give the guilty conscience peace,
  Or wash away one stain.

2 But Christ, the heav'nly Lamb,
  Takes all our sins away;
A sacrifice of nobler name,
  And richer blood than they.

3 My faith would lay its hand
  On that dear head of thine,
While like a penitent I stand,
  And there confess my sin.

4 My soul looks back to see
  The burdens thou didst bear,
When hanging on the cursed tree,
  And hopes her guilt was there.

5 Believing we rejoice
  To see the curse remove;
We bless the Lamb with chearful voice,
  And sing his bleeding love.

HYMN CXXVIII.

A SONNET.

1 AWAKE and sing the song
    Of Moses and the Lamb;
Wake ev'ry heart and ev'ry tongue,
    To praise the Saviour's name.

2 Sing of his dying love,
    Sing of his rising pow'r,
Sing how he interceeds above,
    For those, whose sins he bore.

3 Sing 'till we feel our hearts
    Ascending with our tongue,
Sing 'till the love of sin departs,
    And **grace** inspires our songs.

4 Sing on your heav'nly way,
    Ye ransom'd sinners sing;
Sing on, rejoicing ev'ry day,
    In Christ th' eternal king.

5 Soon shall ye hear him say,
    " Ye blessed children come;"
Soon will he call you hence away,
    And take his wand'rers home.

HYMN CXXIX.

EBEN-EZER. 1 SAM. VII. 12.

1 COME, thou fount of ev'ry blessing!
    Tune my heart to sing thy grace!
Streams of mercy never ceasing,
    Call for songs of loudest praise:
Teach me some melodious sonnet,
    Sung by flaming tongues above;
Praise the mount — I'm fixt upon it,
    Mount of God's unchanging love!

2 Here I raise mine Eben-ezer,
    Hither by thy help I'm come;
And I hope by thy good pleasure,
    Safely to arrive at home:
Jesus sought me, when a stranger
    Wand'ring from the fold of God;
He, to rescue me from danger,
    Interpos'd with precious blood.

3 Oh! to grace how great a debtor,
    Daily I'm constrain'd to be!
Let that grace, Lord, like a fetter,
    Bind my wand'ring heart to thee!
Prone to wander, Lord, I feel it,
    Prone to leave the God I love —
Here's my heart, Lord, take and seal it;
    Seal it from thy courts above!

HYMN CXXX.

LONGING AFTER CHRIST.

1 THOU shepherd of Israel, and mine,
    The joy, and desire of my heart;
For closer communion I pine,
    I long to reside where thou art:
The pasture I languish to find,
    Where all, who their shepherd obey,
Are fed, on thy bosom reclin'd,
    Are screen'd from the heat of the day.

2 Ah! shew me that happiest place,
    That place of thy people's abode;
Where saints in an extacy gaze,
    And hang on a crucify'd God:
Thy love for a sinner declare,
    Thy passion and death on the tree;
My spirit to Calvary bear,
    To suffer, and triumph with thee.

3 'Tis there with the lambs of thy flock,
    There only I covet to rest;
To lie at the foot of the rock,
    Or rise to be hid in thy breast;
'Tis there I wou'd always abide,
    And never a moment depart,
Conceal'd in the cleft of thy side,
    Eternally held in thine heart.

HYMN CXXXI.

CHRIST WITHDRAWN.

1 O What shall I do to retrieve
    The love for a season bestow'd;
'Tis better to die than to live
    Exil'd from the presence of God:
With sorrow distracted and doubt,
    With palpable horror oppreſt,
The city I wander about,
    And seek my repose in his breast.

2 Ye watchmen of Israel, declare
    If ye my beloved have seen,
And point to that heav'nly fair,
    Surpassing the children of men:
My lover and lord from above,
    Who only can quiet my pain,
Whom only I languish to love,
    O where shall find him again?

3 The joy and desire of mine eyes,
    The end of my sorrow and woe;
My hope, and my heav'nly prize,
    My height of ambition below:
Once more if he shew me his face,
    He never again shall depart,
Detain'd in my closest embrace,
    Conceal'd in the depth of my heart.

HYMN CXXXII.

THE PILGRIM's SONG.

1 RISE, my soul, and stretch thy wings,
    Thy better portion trace;
Rise from transitory things,
    Tow'rds heaven, thy native place:
Sun, and moon, and stars decay,
    Time shall soon this earth remove;
Rise, my soul, and haste away,
    To seats prepar'd above.

2 Rivers to the ocean run,
    Nor stay in all their course;
Fire ascending seeks the sun,
    Both speed them to their source:
So a soul that's born of God
    Pants to view his glorious face,
Upward tends to his abode,
    To rest in his embrace.

3 Cease, ye pilgrims, cease to mourn,
    Press onward to the prize;
Soon our Saviour will return,
    Triumphant in the skies:
Yet a season, and you know
    Happy entrance will be giv'n,
All our sorrows left below,
    And earth exchang'd for heav'n.

HYMN CXXXIII.

ANOTHER.

1 CHildren of the heav'nly king,
   As ye journey sweetly sing;
Sing your Saviour's worthy praise,
Glorious in his works and ways!

2 Ye are trav'ling home to God,
In the way the fathers trod:
They are happy now, and ye
Soon their happiness shall see.

3 O ye banish'd seed be glad!
Christ our advocate is made;
Us to save our flesh assumes,
Brother to our souls becomes.

4 Shout ye little flock and blest,
You on Jesu's throne shall rest;
There your seat is now prepar'd,
There your kingdom, and reward.

5 Fear not brethren, joyful stand
On the borders of your land;
Jesus Christ, your father's son,
Bids you undismay'd go on.

6 Lord!

6 Lord! obediently we'll go,
  Gladly leaving all below;
  Only thou our leader be,
  And we still will follow thee!

HYMN CXXXIV.

FLESH AND SPIRIT.

1 WHAT diff'rent pow'rs of grace and sin,
    Attend our mortal state?
  I hate the thoughts that work within,
    And do the works I hate.

2 Now I complain, and groan and die,
    While sin and satan reign;
  Now raise my songs of triumph high,
    For grace prevails again.

3 So darkness struggles with the light,
    'Till perfect day arise;
  Water and fire maintain the fight,
    Until the weaker dies.

4 Thus will the flesh and spirit strive,
    And vex, and break my peace;
  But I shall quit this mortal life,
    And sin for ever cease.

HYMN CXXXV.

THE BEATIFIC VISION.

1 I Long to behold him array'd,
  With glory and light from above;
The king in his beauty display'd
  His beauty of holiest love:
I languish, and die to be there,
  Where Jesus hath fix'd his abode;
O when shall we meet in the air,
  And fly to the mountain of God!

2 With him I on Zion shall stand,
  (For Jesus hath spoken the word)
The breadth of Immanuel's land
  Survey by the light of my Lord:
But when on thy bosom reclin'd,
  Thy face I am strengthen'd to see,
My fulness of rapture I find,
  My heaven of heavens in thee!

3 How happy the people that dwell
  Secure in the city above!
No pain the inhabitants feel,
  No sickness or sorrow shall prove:
Physician of souls unto me,
  Forgiveness and holiness give,
And then from the body set free,
  And then to the city receive.

HYMN CXXXVI.

1 O Jesu, our Lord,
  Thy name be ador'd,
For all the rich blessings convey'd by thy word.

2 In spirit we trace
  Thy wonders of grace,
And chearfully join in a concert of praise.

3 The antient of days
  His glory displays,
And shines on his chosen with cherishing rays.

4 The trumpet of God
  Is sounding abroad,
The language of mercy — salvation thro' blood.

5 Thrice happy are they,
  Who hear and obey,
And share in the blessings of this gospel-day.

6 The people who know
  The Saviour below,
With burning affection to worship him glow.

7   Their anguish and smart,
      And sorrows depart,
   Who find his salvation inscrib'd on their heart.

8   This blessing be mine,
      Thro' favour divine,
   But O, my redeemer, the glory be thine!

9   The work is of grace,
      Thine, thine be the praise;
   And mine to adore thee, and tell of thy ways.

HYMN CXXXVII.

CRUCIFIXION TO THE WORLD.

1 WHEN I survey the wondrous cross,
      On which the prince of glory dy'd,
   My richest gain I count but loss,
      And pour contempt on all my pride.

2 Forbid it, Lord, that I should boast,
      Save in the cross of Christ my God;
   All the vain things that charm me most,
      I sacrifice them to his blood.

O   3 See

3 See from his head, his hands, his feet,
　　Sorrow and love flow mingling down!
　Did e'er such love, such sorrow meet?
　　Or thorns compose so bright a crown?

4 Were the whole realm of nature mine,
　　That were a present far too small;
　Love so amazing, so divine,
　　Demands my soul, my life, my all.

HYMN CXXXVIII.

FAREWEL TO THE WORLD.

1 WORLD, adieu! thou real cheat,
　　Oft have thy deceitful charms
　Fill'd my heart with fond conceit,
　　Foolish hopes, and false alarms:
　Now I see as clear as day,
　How thy follies pass away.

2 Vain thy entertaining sights,
　　False thy promises renew'd,
　All the pomp of thy delights
　　Does but flatter and delude:
　Thee I quit for heav'n above,
　Object of the noblest love.

3 Farewel

3 Farewel honour's empty pride,
  Thy own nice, uncertain guſt,
If the leaſt miſchance betide,
  Lays thee lower than the duſt:
Worldly honours end in gall,
Riſe to-day — to-morrow fall.

4 Fooliſh vanity — farewel —
  More inconſtant than the wave,
Where thy ſoothing fancies dwell,
  Pureſt tempers they deprave:
He, to whom I fly from thee,
Jeſus Chriſt ſhall ſet me free.

5 Let not, Lord, my wand'ring mind
  Follow after fleeting toys,
Since in thee alone I find
  Solid and ſubſtantial joys:
Joys that never over paſt,
Thro' eternity ſhall laſt.

6 Lord, how happy is the heart
  After thee while it aſpires!
True and faithful as thou art,
  Thou ſhalt anſwer its deſires;
It ſhall ſee the glorious ſcene
Of thine everlaſting reign.

HYMN CXXXIX.

GRATITUDE.

1 WHEN all thy mercies, O my God,
    My rising soul surveys,
Transported with the view I'm lost
    In wonder, love, and praise.

2 Thy providence my life sustain'd,
    And all my wants redrest,
When in the silent womb I lay,
    And hung upon the breast.

3 Unnumber'd comforts to my soul
    Thy tender care bestow'd,
Before my infant-heart conceiv'd
    From whom those comforts flow'd.

4 When in the slipp'ry paths of youth,
    With heedless steps I ran;
Thine arm, unseen, convey'd me safe,
    And led me on to man.

5 When worn by sickness, oft hast thou
    With health renew'd my face;
And when in sins and sorrows sunk,
    Reviv'd my soul with grace.

6 Thy bounteous hand with heav'nly bliss,
    Has made my cup run o'er;
And in thy son, my dearest friend,
    Has doubled all my store.

7 Thro' ev'ry period of my life,
    Thy goodness I'll pursue;
And after death in distant worlds,
    The glorious theme renew.

8 When nature fails, and day and night
    Divide thy works no more;
My ever grateful heart, O Lord,
    Thy mercy shall adore.

9 Thro' all eternity to thee
    A joyful song I'll raise;
For oh! eternity's too short
    To utter all thy praise.

HYMN CXL.

1 WHAT shall we render unto thee,
    Thou glorious Lord of life and pow'r!
Teach us to bow the humble knee;
    Teach us with thankfulness t'adore;
To praise thee as thy saints above,
To praise thee for thy wondrous love.

2 When like lost sheep we wander'd wide,
    And left the watchful shepherd's eye;
When borne along th' impetuous tide
    Of this world's sin and vanity;
Our Jesus from the heav'ns came down,
To save us by his grace alone.

3 He bore our sins upon the tree,
    (To seek and save the lost he came)
There was he bound to set us free,
    From death, and everlasting shame:
The captive flock from hell was freed,
And ransom'd when their shepherd bled.

4 Before the father's awful throne,
    Our merciful high-priest he stands,
And interceding for his own,
    The purchas'd remnant now demands;
His people's everlasting friend,
Who loving—loves them to the end.

5 May we his banish'd ones rejoice,
    Him for our Lord and God to own;
To take him as our only choice,
    And cleave to him in love alone;
Be growing up in holiness,
Then meet him in the realms of bliss.

HYMN CXLI.

JOHN XIII. I.

1 THIS God is the God we adore,
    Our faithful unchangeable friend;
Whose love is as great as his pow'r,
    And neither knows measure nor end.

2 'Tis Jesus, the FIRST and the LAST,
    Whose spirit shall guide us safe home;
We'll praise him for all that is past,
    And trust him for all that's to come.

HYMN CXLII.

1 A Thousand foes prepare to war
    Against a feeble saint;
Jesus, in my behalf appear,
    And chear me, lest I faint.

2 Give me an heart divorc'd from sin,
    Shut up from worldly care;
Constant, sincere, and fervent in
    The exercise of pray'r.

3 Watchful

3 Watchful in ev'ry work and word,
   Ready to speak thy praise;
Arm'd with thy Spirit's two-edg'd sword,
   And cloath'd with ev'ry grace.

4 Fill'd with a godly filial fear,
   A constant jealous care;
Lest I from the right path shou'd err,
   Or fall into a snare.

5 To ev'ry earthly object dead;
   Alive to things above;
Conform'd into my living head,
   And fill'd with burning love.

6 Let furious heats no more molest,
   Nor passions chafe my mind;
Quench all ill tempers in my breast,
   And make me meek and kind.

7 Grant me a serious, sober mind,
   From levity set free;
That I may shew to all mankind,
   Thine image, Lord, in me.

8 Assume in me thy dwelling place,
   Thy temple, and thy throne;
Then stubborn self shall bend to grace,
   And antichrist fall down.

HYMN

HYMN CXLIII.

ADORING CHRIST.

1 Brethren let us join to bless
   Jesus Christ, our joy and peace;
   Let our praise to him be giv'n,
   High at God's right hand in heav'n!

2 Master see! to thee we bow,
   Thou art Lord, and only thou;
   Thou the blessed virgin's seed,
   Glory of thy church, and head.

3 Thee the angels ceaseless sing,
   Thee we praise, our priest and king;
   Worthy is thy name of praise,
   Full of glory, full of grace.

4 Thou hast the glad tidings brought,
   Of salvation by thee wrought;
   Wrought for all thy church! and we
   Worship in their company.

5 We thy little flock adore
   Thee, the Lord for evermore!
   Ever with us shew thy love,
   'Till we join with those above!

HYMN CXLIV.

TO THE HOLY GHOST.

1 STAY, thou insulted spirit, stay,
  Tho' I have done thee such despite;
Cast not a sinner quite away,
  Nor take thine everlasting flight.

2 Tho' I have most unfaithful been,
  Of all, whoe'er thy grace receiv'd,
Ten thousand times thy goodness seen,
  Ten thousand times thy goodness griev'd.

3 But O! the chief of sinners spare,
  In honour of my great high-priest;
Nor in thy righteous anger swear
  T'exclude me from thy people's rest.

4 If yet thou canst my sins forgive,
  E'en now, O Lord, relieve my woes;
Into thy rest of love receive,
  And bless me with the calm repose.

5 E'en now my weary soul release,
  And raise me by thy gracious hand;
Guide me into thy perfect peace,
  And bring me to the promis'd land.

HYMN CXLV.

THE CHRISTIAN's EXPECTATION.

1 GOD of all confolation, take
   The glory of thy grace;
Thy gifts to thee we render back
   In ceafelefs fongs of praife.

2 Not unto us, but thee, O Lord,
   Glory to thee be giv'n,
For ev'ry gracious thought and word,
   That brought us nearer heav'n.

3 Our fouls are in his mighty hand,
   And he will keep them ftill;
And you and I fhall furely ftand
   With him on Zion's hill.

4 Him eye to eye we there fhall fee,
   Our face, like his, fhall fhine;
O what a glorious company,
   When faints and angels join!

5 O what a joyful meeting there,
   In robes of white array'd,
Palms in our hands we all fhall bear,
   And crowns upon our head!

6 Then

6 Then let us earnestly contend,
   And fight our passage thro';
Bear in our faithful mind the end,
   And keep the prize in view.

7 Then let us hasten to the day,
   When all shall be brought home;
Come, O redeemer, come away,
   Lord Jesu, quickly come!

HYMN CXLVI.

A BLESSED GOSPEL.

1 BLEST are the souls that hear and know
      The gospel's joyful sound;
  Peace shall attend the path they go,
      And light their steps surround.

2 Their joy shall bear their spirits up,
      Thro' their redeemer's name;
  His righteousness exalts their hope,
      Nor Satan dares condemn.

3 The Lord our glory and defence,
      Strength, and salvation gives;
  Israel, thy king for ever reigns,
      Thy God for ever lives.

HYMN

HYMN CXLVII.

ADORING JESUS.

1 O Come let us join,
    Together combine,
  To praise our dear Saviour, our master divine.

2 Him let us adore,
    Who cover'd with gore,
  Late hanged on Calvary, both wounded and poor.

3 He worthy is blest
    By spirits at rest,
  Who once in this desart his godhead confess'd.

4 The prophets who told
    His suff'rings of old,
  Sing now sweet thankgivings on psalteries of gold.

5 The fathers to whom
    He shew'd he would come,
  Now in his pavilion take up their long home.

6 The spirits of men,
  Who for him were slain,
From Abel the righteous share now in his reign.

7 The apostles who stood,
  Resisting to blood,
For Jesus's gospel rejoice in their God.

8 O church of the Lamb,
  Here met, do the same,
With saints and with angels bless Jesus's name.

9 My soul bear a part,
  For ransom'd thou art,
By Jesu's blood-shedding, his burial, and smart.

10 To him that was slain,
  The scorn'd Nazarene,
Be glory and honour; let all say " Amen."

HYMN CXLVIII.

1 O Thou holy Lamb divine,
    How canst thou and sinners join?
  God of spotless purity,
    How shall man concur with thee?

2 Offer up one sacrifice
Acceptable to the skies;
What shall wretched sinners bring
Pleasing to the glorious king?

3 Only sin we call our own,
But thou art the darling son,
Thine it is our God t'appease,
Him thou dost for ever please.

4 We on thee alone depend,
With thy sacrifice ascend,
Render what thy grace hath giv'n,
Lift our souls with thee to heav'n.

HYMN CXLIX.

HUMAN WEAKNESS AND CHRIST's STRENGTH.

1 LET me but hear my Saviour say,
Strength shall be equal to thy day;
Then I rejoice in deep distress,
Leaning on all sufficient grace.

2 I glory in infirmity,
That Christ's own pow'r may rest on me;
When I am weak, then am I strong,
Grace is my shield, and Christ my song.

HYMN CL.

GOD GLORIOUS AND SINNERS SAVED.

1 FATHER, how wide thy glory shines!
　　How high thy wonders rise!
Known thro' the earth by thousand signs,
　　By thousand thro' the skies.

2 Those mighty orbs proclaim thy pow'r,
　　Their motions speak thy skill;
And on the wings of ev'ry hour
　　We read thy patience still.

3 But when we view thy great design
　　To save rebellious worms;
Where vengeance and compassion join
　　In their divinest forms.

4 Here the whole deity is known,
　　Nor dares a creature guess
Which of the glories brightest shone,
　　The justice, or the grace.

5 Now the full glories of the Lamb
　　Adorn the heav'nly plains,
Bright seraphs learn Immanuel's name,
　　And try their choicest strains.

6 O may

6 O may I bear some humble part
    In that immortal song;
Wonder and joy shall tune my heart,
    And love command my tongue.

HYMN CLI.

THY WORD IS TRUTH.

1 MY hiding place, my refuge, tow'r,
    And shield art thou, O Lord,
I firmly anchor all my hopes
    On thy unerring word.

2 Engrav'd as in eternal brass,
    The mighty promise shines;
Nor can the pow'rs of darkness raze
    Those everlasting lines.

3 The sacred word of grace is strong,
    As that which built the skies;
The voice which rolls the stars along,
    Spake all the promises.

4 My hiding-place, my refuge, tow'r,
    And shield art thou, O Lord,
I firmly anchor all my hopes
    On thy unerring word.

HYMN CLII.

PROV. XXVIII. 14.

1 GOD of all grace and majesty!
    Supremely great and good!
If I have favour found with thee,
    Thro' th' atoning blood:
The guard of all thy mercies give,
    And to my pardon join
A fear, left I shou'd ever grieve
    The gracious spirit divine.

2 If mercy is indeed with thee,
    May I obedient prove,
Nor e'er abuse my liberty,
    Or sin against thy love:
This choicest fruit of faith bestow
    On thy sojourner here;
And let me pass my days below
    In humbleness and fear.

3 Still may I walk as in thy sight,
    My strict observer see;
And thou by rev'rent love unite
    My child-like heart to thee:
Still let me, till my days are past,
    At Jesu's feet abide:
So shall he lift me up at last,
    And seat me by his side.

HYMN CLIII.

JOHN XIII. 9.

1 JESUS, thou art my righteousness,
    For all my sins were thine;
Thy death hath bought of God my peace,
    Thy life hath made him mine:
My dying Saviour, and my God!
    Fountain for guilt and sin!
Sprinkle me ever with thy blood,
    And cleanse, and keep me clean.

2 Wash me, and make me thus thine own,
    Wash me, and mine thou art;
Wash me, but not my feet alone,
    My hands, my head, and heart!
Th' atonement of thy blood apply,
    'Till faith to sight improve;
'Till hope in full enjoyment die,
    And all my soul be love!

HYMN CLIV.

INCONSTANCY.

1 LORD Jesu, when, when shall it be,
    That I no more shall break with thee?
When will this war of passion cease,
And my free soul enjoy thy peace?

2 Here I repent, and sin again;
 Now I revive, and now am slain;
 Slain by the same unhappy dart,
 Which oh! too often wounds my heart.

3 O Saviour, when, when shall I be,
 A garden seal'd to all but thee?
 No more expos'd, no more undone,
 But live and grow to thee alone.

4 Guide thou, O Lord, guide thou my course,
 And draw me on with thy sweet force;
 Still make me walk, still make me tend,
 By thee my way, to God my end.

HYMN CLV.

TO JESUS CHRIST.

1 HOLY Lamb, who thee receive,
 Who in thee begin to live;
 Day and night they cry to thee,
 As thou art, so let us be.

2 Fix, O fix my wav'ring mind,
 To thy cross my spirit bind;
 Earthly passions far remove,
 Perfect all our souls in love.

3 Dust and ashes tho' we be,
 Full of guilt, and misery;
 Thine we are, thou son of God,
 Take the purchase of thy blood.

4 Boundless wisdom, pow'r divine,
 Love unspeakable, are thine;
 Praise by all to thee be giv'n,
 Sons of earth, and hosts of heav'n!

HYMN CLVII.

COMPLEATNESS IN CHRIST.

1 KIND is the speech of Christ our Lord,
 Affection sounds in ev'ry word;
 " Thou art my chosen one, he cries,
 Bound to my heart by various ties."

2 Sweet is thy voice, dear Lord, to me,
 " I will behold no spot in thee;"
 What mighty wonders love performs,
 That puts a comeliness on worms!

3 Defil'd and loathsome as we are,
 Thou mak'st us white, and call'st us fair!
 Adorn'st us with thy heav'nly dress,
 Thy graces, and thy righteousness.

4 O may my spirit daily rise
   On wings of faith above the skies;
   'Till death shall make my last remove,
   To dwell for ever in thy love!

HYMN CLVI.

PRESERVING GRACE.

1 TO God the only wise,
      Our Saviour and our king,
   Let all the saints below the skies
      Their humble praises bring.

2 'Tis his almighty love,
      His council and his care,
   Preserves us safe from sin and death,
      And ev'ry hurtful snare.

3 He will present our souls
      Unblemish'd, and compleat,
   Before the glory of his face,
      With joys divinely great.

4 Then all the chosen seed
      Shall meet around the throne;
   Shall bless the conduct of his grace,
      And make his wonders known.

5 To our redeeming God
     Wisdom and pow'r belongs,
   Immortal crowns of majesty,
     And everlasting songs.

HYMN CLVIII.

PLEADING THE COVENANT.

1 O Lord my God, whose sov'reign love
    Is still the same, nor e'er can move;
  Look to the covenant, and see
  For once thy love was shewn to me:
    Remember, O my dearest friend,
    And love me alway to the end.

2 Be with me still, as heretofore,
  And help me forward more and more,
  My strong, my stubborn will incline
  To be obedient still to thine:
    O lead me by thy gracious hand,
    And guide me safe to Canaan's land.

3 I need not say, for well thou know'st
  How I, without thy help I'm lost;
  Thou know'st how apt I am to err,
  But thou canst make me persevere:
    Be then my light, and let me see
    That I have yet my lot in thee.

4 O take

4 O take me up above the skies,
   Translate me to thy paradise;
Then shall I rest from ev'ry woe,
From all the troubles here below:
   Grant this, my Lord, and kindly say,
   Come, my redeemed, come away.

HYMN CLIX.

JOB V. 19.

1 WHY should I doubt his love at last,
   With anxious thoughts perplext?
Who sav'd me in the troubles past,
   Will save me in the next:
Will save, 'till at my latest hour,
   With more than conquest blest.
I soar beyond temptations pow'r,
   To my redeemer's breast.

HYMN CLX.

GOD's OMNIPRESCIENCE.

1 LORD, all I am is known to thee,
   In vain my soul would try
To shun thy presence, or to flee
   The notice of thine eye.

2 Thy

2 Thy all-surrounding sight surveys
    My rising and my rest,
My public walks, my private ways,
    The secrets of my breast.

3 My thoughts lie open to thee, Lord,
    Before they're form'd within,
And e're my lips pronounce the word,
    Thou know'st the sense I mean.

4 O wondrous knowledge, deep and high!
    Where can a creature hide?
Within thy circling arms I lie,
    Beset on ev'ry side.

5 So let my grace surround me still,
    And like a bulwark prove,
To guard my soul from ev'ry ill,
    Secur'd by sov'reign love.

HYMN CLXI.

THANKSGIVING.

1 BLESS, O my soul, the living God,
   Call home thy thoughts that rove abroad;
Let all the pow'rs within me join,
In work and worship so divine.

2 Bless, O my soul, the God of grace,
His favours claim thy highest praise;
Why should the wonders he hath wrought
Be lost in silence, and forgot?

3 'Twas he, my soul, that sent his son
To die for crimes which thou hast done;
He owns the ransom, and forgives
The hourly follies of our lives.

4 Our youth decay'd, his pow'r repairs,
His mercy crowns our growing years;
He satisfies our mouth with good,
And fills our mouth with heav'nly food.

5 Let the whole earth his pow'r confess,
Let the whole earth adore his grace;
May all our pow'rs within us join,
In work and worship so divine!

HYMN CLXII.

SIGHT OF GOD AND CHRIST IN HEAVEN.

1 DEscend from heav'n, immortal dove,
Stoop down and take us on thy wings,
And mount, and bear us far above
The reach of these inferior things.

2 O for a sight, a pleasing sight!
Of our almighty father's throne!
There sits our Saviour, crown'd with light,
Cloath'd in a body like our own.

3 Adoring saints around him stand,
And thrones and pow'rs before him fall,
The God shines gracious thro' the man,
And sheds sweet glories on them all.

4 When shall the day, dear Lord appear,
That we shall mount to dwell above,
And stand and bow amongst them there,
And view thy face, and sing thy love.

HYMN CLXIII.

LOOKING TO JESUS.

1 HOW glorious the Lamb
   Is seen on the throne!
His labours are o'er,
   His conquests are won.
A kingdom is given
   Into the Lamb's hand,
In earth and in heaven,
   For ever to stand.

2 Ye finners below
   Then truft in the Lord,
Look up to his arm,
   His honour, his word:
Athirft for his favour,
   His godhead adore,
Look up to your Saviour,
   And joy evermore!

PARTICULAR

PSALMS

SELECTED FROM THE

OLD VERSION.

PSALM I.

1. THE man is blest, that hath not lent
   To wicked men his ear;
Nor led his life as sinners do,
   Nor sat in scorners chair.

2. But in the law of God the Lord
   Doth set his whole delight;
And in the same doth exercise
   Himself both day and night.

3 He shall be like a tree that is
 Planted the rivers nigh ;
Which in due season bringeth forth
 Its fruit abundantly.

4 Whose leaf shall never fade nor fall,
 But flourishing shall stand :
E'en so all things shall prosper well,
 That this man takes in hand.

5 As for ungodly men, with them
 It shall be nothing so ;
But as the chaff, which by the wind
 Is driven to and fro'.

6 Therefore the wicked man shall not
 In judgment stand upright ;
Nor in th' assembly of the just
 Shall sinners come in sight.

7 Foy why ? the way of godly men
 Unto the Lord is known :
Whereas the way of wicked men
 Shall quite be overthrown.

PSALM V.

VERSES 1.—4, 11.

1 INcline thine ears, O Lord, and let
    My words have free access
To thee, who art my God and king,
    From whom I seek redress.

2 Hear me betimes, Lord, tarry not,
    For I will have respect,
My supplication night and morn,
    To thee will I direct.

3 And I will patiently still trust
    In thee my God alone:
Thou art not pleas'd with wickedness,
    And ill with thee dwells none.

4 Such as be foolish shall not stand
    In sight of thee, O Lord:
Vain workers of iniquity
    Thou always hast abhorr'd.

5 But thou with favour wilt increase
    The just and righteous still;
And with thy grace, as with a shield,
    Defend him from all ill.

PSALM VIII.

VERSES 1—4, 8.

1 O Lord our God, how wonderful
    Are thy works ev'ry where;
  Thy fame furmounts in dignity
    The higheſt heav'ns that are.

2 E'en by the mouths of fucking babes
    Thou wilt confound thy foes;
  For in thoſe babes thy might is feen,
    Thy graces they difcloſe.

3 And when I fee the heav'ns above,
    The work of thine own hand;
  The fun, the moon, and all the ſtars,
    In order as they ſtand.

4 Lord what is man, that thou of him
    Tak'ſt fuch abundant care?
  Or what's the fon of man, whom thou
    To viſit doſt not fpare?

5 O Lord our God, how excellent
    Is thy moſt glorious name
  In all the earth! therefore we do
    Praiſe and adore the fame.

PSALM XV.

VERSES 1—5, 7.

1 Within thy tabernacle, Lord,
    Who shall inhabit still?
Or whom wilt thou receive to dwell
    In thy most holy hill?

2 The man whose life is uncorrupt,
    Whose works are just and strait;
Whose heart doth think the very truth,
    And tongue speaks no deceit.

3 That to his neighbour doth no ill
    In body, goods, or name;
Nor willingly doth slanders raise,
    Which might impair the fame.

4 That in his heart regardeth not
    Malicious wicked men:
But those that love and fear the Lord,
    He maketh much of them.

5 His oath, and all his promises
    That keepeth faithfully,
Altho he make his cov'nant so,
    That he doth lose thereby.

6 Whoso doth these things faithfully,
    And turneth not therefrom;
Shall never perish in this world,
    Nor that which is to come.

PSALM XIX.

VERSES 7—14.

1 HOW perfect is the law of God?
    His covenant is sure;
Converting souls, and making wise
    The simple, and obscure.

2 The Lord's commands are righteous, and
    Rejoice the heart; likewise
His precepts are most pure, and do
    Give light unto the eyes.

3 The fear of God is excellent,
    And ever doth endure;
The judgments of the Lord, also
    Most righteous are, and pure.

4 And more to be desired are
    Than much fine gold alway;
The honey and the honey-comb
    Are not so sweet as they.

5 By them thy servant is forwarn'd
   To have God in regard;
And in performance of the same
   There shall be great reward.

6 But Lord, what earthly man doth know
   The errors of his life?
Lord cleanse me from my secret sins,
   Which are in me most rife.

7 And keep me that presumptuous sins
   Prevail not over me;
And so shall I be innocent,
   And great offences flee.

8 Accept my mouth and heart also,
   My words and thoughts each one;
For my Redeemer and my strength,
   O Lord, thou art alone.

PSALM XXIII.

1 MY shepherd is the living Lord,
   Nothing therefore I need;
In pastures fair, near pleasant streams,
   He setteth me to feed.

2 He shall convert and glad my soul
   And bring my mind in frame,
To walk in paths of righteousness,
   For his most holy name.

3 Yea tho' I walk in vale of death,
      Yet will I fear no ill:
Thy rod and staff do comfort me,
      And thou art with me still.

4 And in the presence of my foes
      My table thou shalt spread:
Thou wilt fill full my cup, and thou
      Anointed hast my head.

5 Thro' all my life thy favour is
      So frankly shew'd to me;
That in thy house for evermore
      My dwelling place shall be.

PSALM XXIV.

VERSE 3—6.

1 WHO is the man, O Lord, that shall
      Ascend unto thy hill?
Or pass into thy holy place,
      There to continue still?

2 Ev'n he, whose hands and heart are pure,
      Which nothing doth defile:
His soul not set on vanity,
      And hath not sworn to guile.

3 Him that is such a one, the Lord
    Most highly will regard;
And from his God and Saviour shall
    Receive a just reward.

4 This is the generation of
    Them that do seek his grace;
Ev'n them that with an upright heart,
    O Jacob, seek thy face.

PSALM XXV.

VERSES 4—10.

1 DIRECT me in thy truth,
    And teach me I thee pray;
Thou art my Saviour, and my God,
    On thee I wait alway.

2 Thy mercies manifold
    Remember, Lord, I pray;
In pity thou art plentiful,
    And so hast been alway.

3 Remember not the faults,
    And frailty of my youth;
Call not to mind how ignorant
    I have been of thy truth.

4 Nor after my deserts
   Let me thy mercy find;
But of thine own benignity,
   Lord, have me in thy mind.

5 His mercy is most sweet,
   His truth a perfect guide;
Therefore the Lord will sinners teach,
   And such as go aside.

6 The humble he will teach
   His precepts to obey;
He will direct in all his paths
   The lowly man alway.

7 For all the ways of God
   Both truth and mercy are,
To them that do his covenant,
   And statutes keep with care.

PSALM XXX.

VERSES 1—4.

1 ALL laud and praise with heart and voice,
      O Lord, I give to thee:
Who didst not make my foes rejoice,
   But hast exalted me.

2 O

2 O Lord my God, to thee I cry'd
   In all my pain and grief;
Thou gav'st an ear, and didst provide
   To ease me with relief.

3 Thou Lord, hast brought my soul from hell,
   And thou the same didst save
From them that in the pit do dwell,
   And kept'st me from the grave.

4 Sing praise, ye saints, that prove and see
   The goodness of the Lord;
In honour of his majesty
   Rejoice with one accord.

PSALM XXXIII.

VERSES 1, 3, 4, 7.

1 YE righteous, in the Lord rejoice,
      It is a seemly sight,
That upright men with thankful voice,
   Should praise the Lord of might.

2 Sing to the Lord a song most new,
   With courage give him praise;
For why? his word is ever true
   His works, and all his ways.

3 Both judgment, equity, and right,
    He ever lov'd, and will;
And with his gifts he doth delight
    The earth throughout to fill.

4 Let all the earth then fear the Lord,
    And keep his righteous law;
And all the world, with one accord,
    Dread him and stand in awe.

PSALM XXXIV.

VERSES 1—4, 21.

1 I Will give laud and honour both
    Unto the Lord always;
My mouth also for evermore,
    Shall speak unto his praise.

2 I do delight to laud the Lord
    In soul, in heart, and voice;
That humble men may hear thereof,
    And heartily rejoice.

3 Therefore see that ye magnify
    With me the living Lord;
Let us exalt his holy name
    Always with one accord.

4 For I myself besought the Lord,
    He answer'd me again;
And me deliver'd speedily,
    From all my fear and pain.

5 For they that fear the living Lord
    Are ever safe and sound;
And as for those that trust in him,
    Nothing shall them confound.

PSALM XL.

VERSES 1—4, 15.

1 I Waited long, and sought the Lord,
    And patiently did bear;
At length to me he did accord
    My voice and cry to hear.

2 He brought me from the dreadful pit,
    Out of the mire and clay;
Upon a rock he set my feet,
    And he did guide my way.

3 To me he taught a psalm of praise,
    Which I must shew abroad;
And sing new songs of thanks always
    Unto the Lord my God.

4 When all the folk these things shall see,
    As people much afraid;
Then they unto the Lord will flee,
    And trust upon his aid.

5 Thy tender mercy, Lord, from me
    Withdraw thou not away;
But let thy love and verity
    Preserve me night and day.

PSALM XCII.

VERSES 1, 2, 4, 5, 6, 15.

1 IT is a thing both good and meet,
    To praise the highest Lord;
And to thy name, O thou most high,
    To sing with one accord.

2 To shew the kindness of the Lord,
    Before the day be light;
And to declare his truth abroad,
    When it doth draw to night.

3 For thou hast made me to rejoice
    In things so wrought by thee,
That I have joy in heart and voice
    Thy handy works to see.

4 O Lord, how glorious and how great
    Are thy works round about!
So deeply are thy counsels set,
    That none can find them out.

5 The man unwise cannot tell how
    This work to pass to bring;
And fools also are most unfit
    To understand this thing.

6 The Lord my God is good and just,
    And upright in his will:
He is my rock, my hope, my trust,
    In him there is no ill.

PSALM XCVI.

VERSES 1—4.

1 SING ye with praise unto the Lord,
    New songs with joy and mirth;
Sing unto him with one accord,
    All people on the earth.

2 Yea, sing unto the Lord alway,
    Praise ye his holy name;
Declare, and shew from day to day,
    Salvation by the same.

3 Among the people all declare
    His honour round about;
  To ſhew his wonders do not ſpare
    In all the world throughout.

4 For why? the Lord is much of might,
    And worthy of all praiſe;
  And he is to be dread of right,
    Above all gods always.

PSALM C.

1 ALL people that on earth do dwell,
    Sing to the Lord with chearful voice;
  Him ſerve with fear, his praiſe forth tell,
  Come ye before him and rejoice.

2 The Lord, ye know, is God indeed,
  Without our aid he did us make;
  We are his flock, he doth us feed,
  And for his ſheep he doth us take.

3 O enter then his gates with praiſe,
  Approach with joy his courts unto;
  Praiſe, laud, and bleſs his name always,
  For it is ſeemly ſo to do.

4 For

4 For why? the Lord our God is good,
    His mercy is for ever sure;
    His truth at all times firmly stood,
    And shall from age to age endure.

PSALM CIII.

VERSES 1—4.

1 MY soul, give laud unto the Lord,
    My spirit do the same;
  And all the secrets of my heart,
    Praise ye his holy name.

2 Praise thou the Lord, my soul, who hath
    To thee been very kind;
  And suffer not his benefits
    To slip out of thy mind.

3 That gave thee pardon for thy faults,
    And thee restor'd again,
  From all thy weak and frail disease,
    And heal'd thee of thy pain.

4 That did redeem thy life from death,
    From which thou could'st not flee:
  His mercy and compassion both
    He did extend to thee.

VENI

VENI CREATOR.

VERSES 7—11.

1 O Holy Ghost, into our souls
    Send down thy heav'nly light;
Inflame our hearts with fervent love,
    To serve God day and night.

2 Our weakness strengthen and confirm,
    Which feeble is and frail;
That neither devil, world, nor flesh,
    Against us may prevail.

3 Our enemies put far from us,
    And grant us to obtain
Peace in our hearts with God and man,
    The best and truest gain.

4 And grant, O Lord, that thou being
    Our leader and our guide;
We may avoid the snares of sin,
    And never from thee slide.

5 To us such plenty of thy grace,
    Good Lord, grant we thee pray;
That thou mayst be our comforter,
    At the last dreadful day.

THE LAMENTATION OF A SINNER.

VERSES 1—4, 10, 11.

1 O Lord, turn not thy face away
    From him that lies proſtrate,
Lamenting ſore his ſinful life
    Before thy mercy gate.

2 Which thou doſt open wide to thoſe,
    That do lament their ſin;
O ſhut it not againſt me, Lord,
    But let me enter in.

3 Call me not to a ſtrict account
    How I have lived here;
For then I know right well, O Lord,
    Moſt vile I ſhall appear.

4 I need not to confeſs my life,
    For ſurely thou canſt tell
What I have been, and what I am,
    O Lord, thou knoweſt well.

5 O Lord, I need not to repeat
    What I do beg or crave;
For thou doſt know before I aſk,
    The thing that I would have.

6 Mercy, good Lord, mercy I afk,
　　This is the total fum;
For mercy, Lord, is all my fuit,
　　O let thy mercy come.

SACRAMENTAL HYMNS,

WITH A SMALL COLLECTION

FOR

FESTIVALS

AND

PARTICULAR OCCASIONS.

SACRAMENTAL HYMNS.

HYMN I.

1 THIS day the Lord of hosts invites
    Unto a costly feast;
I wou'd take care, and well prepare
    To be a welcome guest.

2 Awake repentance, faith, and love,
    Awake O ev'ry grace;
To meet your Lord, with one accord,
    In his most holy place.

3 Worldly distraction, stay behind,
    Below the mount abide;
Cause no disturbance in my mind,
    To make my Saviour chide.

4 O come, my Lord, the time draws nigh,
    That I am to receive;
Stand with my pardon sealed by,
    Persuade me to believe.

5 Let not my Jesus now be strange,
   Nor hide himself from me;
But cause thy face to shine upon
   The soul that longs for thee.

6 Come, blessed Spirit, from above,
   My soul do thou inspire,
T' approach the table of the Lord,
   With fulness of desire.

7 O let our entertainment now
   Be so exceeding sweet,
That we may long to come again,
   And at thine altar meet.

HYMN II.

FOR THE LOVE OF CHRIST.

1 COME, dearest Lord, descend and dwell,
   By faith and love in ev'ry breast!
Then shall we know, and taste, and feel,
The joys that cannot be express'd.

2 Come fill our hearts with inward strength,
   Make our enlarged souls possess,
   And learn the heighth, and breadth, and length
   Of thine unmeasurable grace.

3 Now to the God, whose pow'r can do,
More than our thought and wishes know;
Be everlasting honours done,
By all the church, thro' Christ the son.

HYMN III.

PLEADING CHRIST.

1 FATHER, God, who see'st in me
Only sin and misery,
See thine own anointed one,
Look on thy beloved son.

2 Turn from me thy glorious eyes,
To that bloody sacrifice;
To that full atonement made,
To that utmost ransom paid.

3 To the blood that speaks above,
Calls for thy forgiving love;
To the tokens of his death,
Here exhibited beneath.

4 Hear his blood's prevailing cry,
Let thy bowels then reply;
Then thro' him the sinner see;
Then in Jesus look on me!

HYMN IV.

TO CHRIST.

1 LAMB of God, for whom we languish,
   Make thy grief
    Our relief,
 Ease us by thine anguish.

2 O our agonizing Saviour!
   By thy pain
   Let us gain
 God's eternal favour!

3 In thine own appointment bless us,
   Meet us here,
   Now appear
 Our almighty Jesus!

4 Let the ordinance be sealing,
   Enter now,
   Claim us thou,
 For thy constant dwelling.

5 Fill the heart of each believer;
   We are thine,
   Love divine,
 Reign in us for ever.

HYMN V.

ASSURANCE OF PARDON.

1 LORD, how divine thy comforts are!
    How heav'nly is the place,
Where Jesus spreads the sacred feast
    Of his redeeming grace!

2 Here (says the kind redeeming Lord,
    And shews his wounded side)
See here the spring of all your joys,
    That open'd when I dy'd!

3 He smiles, and chears my mournful heart,
    And tells of all his pain;
All this, says he, I bore for thee,
    And then he smiles again.

4 What shall we pay our heav'nly king,
    For grace so vast as this?
He brings our pardon to our eyes,
    And seals it with a kiss.

5 Let such amazing loves as these
    Be sounded all abroad,
Such favours are beyond degrees,
    And worthy of a God.

6 To him, that wash'd us in his blood,
   Be everlasting praise,
Salvation, honour, glory, pow'r,
   Eternal as his days.

HYMN VI.

1 JESU, dear redeeming Lord,
   Magnify thy dying word,
In thine ordinance appear,
Come and meet thy foll'wers here.

2 In the rite thou hast enjoin'd,
Let us now our Saviour find,
Drink thy blood for sinners shed,
Taste thee in the broken bread.

3 Thou our faithful hearts prepare,
Thou thy pard'ning grace declare,
Thou that hast for sinners dy'd,
Shew thyself the crucify'd!

4 All the pow'r of sin remove,
Fill us with thy heav'nly love,
Stamp us with the stamp divine,
Seal us, Lord, for ever thine.

HYMN VII.

THE TRIUMPHAL FEAST.

1 THE Lord, how glorious is his face?
    How kind his smiles appear!
And oh! what melting words he says,
    To ev'ry humble ear!

2 For you, the children of my love,
    It was for you I dy'd;
Behold my bleeding hands and feet,
    And look into my side.

3 These are the wounds for you I bore,
    The tokens of my pains,
When I came down to free your souls,
    From misery and chains.

4 Justice unsheath'd its fiery sword,
    And plung'd it in my heart;
Infinite pangs for you I bore,
    And most tormenting smart.

5 When hell and all its spiteful pow'rs
    Stood dreadful in my way;
To rescue those dear lives of yours,
    I gave my own away.

6 But while I bled, and groan'd, and dy'd,
   I ruin'd Satan's throne;
High on my cross I hung, and spy'd
   The monster tumbling down.

7 Victorious God, what can we pay
   For favours so divine?
Here, Lord, we give our souls away,
   To be for ever thine.

HYMN VIII.

ISAIAH LIII, 6.

1 ARISE, my soul, with wonder see,
   What love divine for thee hath done;
Behold thy sorrow, sin, and grief,
Are laid on God's eternal son.

2 See! from his head, his hands, his feet,
Sorrow and love flow mingling down,
Did e'er such love such sorrow meet,
Or thorns compose so bright a crown?

3 Were the whole realm of nature mine,
That were a present far too small;
Love so amazing, so divine,
Demands my soul, my life, my all.

HYMN IX.

1 GOD of all-redeeming grace,
   By thy pard'ning love compell'd,
Up to thee our souls we raise,
   Up to thee our bodies yield.

2 Thou our sacrifice receive,
   Acceptable thro' thy son;
While to thee alone we live,
   While we die to thee alone.

3 Just it is, and good and right,
   That we shou'd be wholly thine,
In thine only will delight,
   In thy blessed service join.

4 O that ev'ry thought and word
   Might proclaim how good thou art;
Holiness unto the Lord,
   Still be written on our heart!

HYMN X.

1 TOgether with these symbols, Lord,
   Thy blessed self impart;
And let thy very flesh and blood
   Feed the believing heart.

2 Let us from all our sins be wash'd
    In thy redeeming blood;
And let thy spirit be the seal,
    That we are sons of God.

3 Come holy Ghost with Jesu's love,
    Prepare us for this feast;
And let us banquet with our Lord,
    And lean upon his breast.

HYMN XI.

1 ALL praise to the Lord,
    All praise is his due,
To day is his word
    Of promise found true;
We, we are the nations
    Presented to God;
Well pleasing oblations
    Thro' Jesus's blood.

2 Poor Gentiles from far
    To Jesus we came,
And offer'd we are
    To God thro' his name;
To God thro' the spirit
    Ourselves do we give,
And sav'd by the merit
    Of Jesus we live.

HYMN XII.

1 OUR shepherd alone,
    The Lord let us bless,
Who sits on the throne,
    The prince of our peace;
Who evermore saves us
    By shedding his blood;
All hail, holy Jesus,
    Our Lord, and our God!

2 We daily will sing
    Thy merits and praise,
Thou merciful spring
    Of pity and grace:
Thy kindness for ever
    To men we will tell,
And say our dear Saviour
    Redeems us from hell.

3 Preserve us in love
    While here we abide,
Nor ever remove,
    Nor cover, nor hide
Thy glorious salvation,
    'Till joyful we see
The beautiful vision
    Compleated in thee!

HYMN XIII.

CHRIST OUR PASSOVER.

1 THOU very paschal Lamb,
 Whose blood for us was shed,
Thro' whom we out of Egypt came,
 Thy ransom'd people lead!

2 Angel of gospel-grace,
 Fulfil thy character;
To guard and feed thy chosen race,
 In Israel's camp appear.

3 Throughout the desart-way
 Conduct us by thy light!
Be thou a cooling cloud by day,
 A chearing fire by night.

4 Our fainting souls sustain
 With blessings from above,
And ever on thy people rain
 The manna of thy love.

HYMN XIV.

1 JESUS invites his saints
    To meet around his board;
Here pardon'd rebels sit and hold
    Communion with their Lord.

2 For food he gives his flesh,
    He bids us drink his blood;
Amazing favour! matchless grace
    Of our descending God!

3 Let all our pow'rs be join'd,
    His glorious name to raise;
Pleasure and love fill ev'ry mind,
    And ev'ry voice be praise.

HYMN XV.

1 O Jesus, my hope,
    For me offer'd up,
Who with clamour pursu'd thee
    To Calvary's top.

2 The blood thou hast shed,
    For me let it plead,
And declare thou hast dy'd
    In thy murd'rer's stead.

3 Thy

3   Thy blood, which alone
      For sin cou'd atone,
   For the infinite evil
      I madly have done.

4   That only can seal
      My pardon, and fill
   My heart with a pow'r
      Of obeying thy will.

5   Now, now let me know
      It's virtue below,
   Let it wash me, and I
      Shall be whiter than snow.

6   Let it hallow my heart,
      And throughly convert,
   And make me, O Lord,
      In this world as thou art.

7   Each moment apply'd
      My weakness to hide,
   Thy blood be upon me,
      And always abide.

8   My advocate prove
      With the father above,
   And speak me at last
      To the throne of thy love.

HYMN

HYMN XVI.

DEDICATION TO GOD.

1 ALL glory and praise
  To th' antient of days
Who was born and was slain
  To redeem a lost race.

2 Salvation to God,
  Who carry'd our load,
And purchas'd our peace
  With the price of his blood.

3 And shall he not have
  The lives which he gave.
Such an infinite ransom
  For ever to save?

4 Yes, Lord, we are thine,
  And gladly resign
Our souls to be fill'd
  With the fulness divine.

5 We yield thee thine own,
  We'd serve thee alone,
Thy will upon earth
  As in heav'n be done.

6   How, when it shall be
        We cannot foresee;
But oh! let us live,
        Let us die unto thee!

HYMN XVII.

1 THANKFUL for our ev'ry blessing,
        Let us sing
          Christ the spring,
Never, never ceasing!

2 Source of all our gifts and graces,
        Christ we own,
          Christ alone
Calls for all our praises.

3 He dispels our sin and sadness,
        Life imparts,
          Chears our hearts,
Fills with food and gladness.

4 He himself for us hath given,
        Us he feeds,
          Us he leads
To a feast in heaven.

HYMN XVIII.

1 FATHER of mankind,
   Be ever ador'd;
Thy mercy we find
   In sending our Lord,
To ransom and bless us;
   Thy goodness we praise
For sending in Jesus
   Salvation by grace.

2 O son of his love,
   Who designedst to die,
Our curse to remove,
   Our pardon to buy;
Accept our thanksgiving,
   Almighty to save,
Who openest heaven
   To all that believe.

3 O spirit of love,
   Of health and of pow'r,
Thy working we prove,
   Thy grace we adore:
Whose inward revealing
   Applies our Lord's blood,
Attesting and sealing
   Us children of God.

HYMN XIX.

CALVARY.

1 LAMB of God, whose bleeding love
    We now recal to mind,
Send the answer from above,
    And let us mercy find:
Think on us who think on thee,
    And ev'ry strugling soul release:
O remember Calvary,
    And bid us go in peace.

2 By thine agonizing pain,
    And bloody sweat, we pray;
By thy dying love to man,
    Take all our sins away:
Burst our bonds, and set us free,
    From all iniquity release:
O remember, &c.

3 Let thy blood by faith apply'd,
    The sinner's pardon seal;
Speak us freely justify'd,
    And all our sickness heal.
By thy passion on the tree,
    Let all our griefs and troubles cease;
O remember, &c.

4 Never would we hence depart,
    Till thou our wants relieve;
Write forgiveness on our hearts,
    And all thine image give.
Still our souls shall cry to thee,
    'Till all renew'd in holiness;
O remember Calvary,
    And bid us go in peace.

HYMN XX.

1 WE sing th' amazing deeds
    That grace divine performs;
Th' eternal God comes down and bleeds,
    To nourish dying worms.

2 Th' angelic host above
    Did never taste this food;
They feast upon their maker's love
    But not a Saviour's blood.

3 Salvation to the name
    Of our adored Christ;
Thro' the wide earth his grace proclaim,
    His glory in the high'st.

HYMN XXI.

1 JESU, suff'ring deity,
 Can we help rememb'ring thee,
 Thee, whose blood for us did flow,
 Thee, who savedst us from woe!

2 Thee, redeemer of mankind,
 Gladly now we call to mind;
 Thankfully the grace approve,
 Take the tokens of thy love.

3 Thus for thy dear sake we do,
 Here thy bloody passion shew,
 Till thou dost to judgment come
 Till thy arms receive us home.

HYMN XXII.

1 OUR lives, our blood we here present,
 If for thy sake they may be spent;
 Fulfil thy sov'reign council, Lord,
 Thy will be done, thy name ador'd.

2 Give us thy strength, thou God of pow'r,
 Then let men scorn, and satan roar;
 Thy faithful witnesses we'll be:
 'Tis fix'd — we can do all thro' thee.

HYMN XXIII.

1 COME, O my soul, and sing
  How Jesus hath thee fed;
How Jesus gave himself for thee,
  The true and living bread.

2 I love my Saviour Christ;
  His grace did freely move,
And justly my affections claim,
  I cannot help but love.

3 I love thee, O my Lord,
  I gladly thee adore;
O may I never turn again!
  But love thee more and more.

4 O raise my feeble flame,
  My little stock improve;
Increase my ardour day by day,
  And change me all to love.

HYMN XXIV.

1 SITTING around our father's board,
  We raise our tuneful breath;
Our faith beholds our dying Lord,
  And dooms our sins to death.

2 We see the blood of Jesus shed,
    Whence all our pardons rise;
The sinner views th' atonement made,
    And loves the sacrifice.

3 Oh! 'tis impossible that we,
    Who dwell in feeble clay,
Should equal suff'rings bear for thee,
    Or equal thanks repay.

HYMNS FOR SOCIETIES.

HYMN XXV.

BREATHING AFTER THE SPIRIT.

1 COME, holy Spirit, heav'nly dove,
 With all thy quick'ning pow'rs;
Kindle a flame of sacred love,
 In these cold hearts of ours.

2 See how we grovel here below,
 Fond of these earthly toys;
Our souls how heavily they go,
 To reach eternal joys!

3 In vain we tune our formal songs,
 In vain we strive to rise;
Hosannas languish on our tongues,
 And our devotion dies.

4 Dear Lord, and shall we ever live
    At this poor dying rate?
Our love so faint, so cold to thee,
    And thine to us so great?

5 Come, holy Spirit, heav'nly dove,
    With all thy quick'ning pow'rs;
Come shed abroad a Saviour's love,
    And that shall kindle ours.

HYMN XXVI.

CHRISTIAN FELLOWSHIP.

1 TRY us, O God, and search the ground
    Of ev'ry sinful heart;
Whate'er of sin in us is found,
    O bid it all depart!

2 When to the right or left we stray,
    Leave us not comfortless:
But guide our feet into the way
    Of everlasting peace.

3 Help us to help each other, Lord,
    Each other's cross to bear;
Let each his friendly aid afford,
    And feel another's care.

4 Help us to build each other up,
　　Our little stock improve;
　Increase our faith, confirm our hope,
　　And perfect us in love.

5 Then, when the mighty work is wrought,
　　Receive thy ready bride;
　Give us in heav'n an happy lot,
　　With all the sanctify'd.

HYMN XXVII.

THE SAME.

1 JESU, Lord, we look to thee,
　Let us in thy name agree,
　Shew thyself the prince of peace,
　Bid all jarrs for ever cease.

2 By thy reconciling love
　Ev'ry stumbling block remove;
　Each to each unite, endear,
　Come, and spread thy banner here.

3 Make us of one heart and mind,
　Courteous, pityful, and kind,
　Lowly, meek in thought and word,
　Altogether like our Lord.

4 Let us each for other care,
  Each another's burden bear;
  To thy church the pattern give,
  Shew how true believers live!

5 Let us then with joy remove
  To thy family above,
  On the wings of angels fly,
  Shew how true believers die!

HYMN XXVIII.

1 STILL, O Lord, our faith increase,
  Cleanse from all unrighteousness;
  Thee th' unholy cannot see,
  Make, O make us meet for thee!
  Ev'ry vile affection kill,
  Free our souls from ev'ry ill,
  Conquer ev'ry reigning sin,
  Write thy law of love within.

2 Hence may all our actions flow,
  Love the proof that Christ we know;
  Mutual love the token be,
  Lord, that we belong to thee!
  Love, thine image, love impart,
  Stamp it on each face and heart;
  Only love to us be giv'n,
  Lord, we ask no other heav'n.

HYMN XXIX.

1 JESU, we thy promise claim,
   We are met in thy dear name,
In the midst do thou appear,
Manifest thy presence here:
Sanctify us, Lord, and bless,
Breathe thy Spirit, give thy peace,
Come descend, celestial dove,
Make this time a time of love.

2 Let the fruits of grace abound,
Let us in thy bowels found;
Faith, and love, and joy increase,
Temperance, and gentleness:
Plant in us thy humble mind,
Patient, pitiful and kind;
Meek and lowly let us be,
Full of goodness, full of thee.

3 Make us all in thee compleat,
Make us all for glory meet;
Meet t' appear before thy sight,
Partners with the saints in light:
Call, O call us each by name,
To the marriage of the Lamb;
Let us lean upon thy breast,
Love be there our endless feast.

HYMN XXX.

1 COME, descend, O heav'nly spirit,
    Fan each spark into a flame;
Blessings let us now inherit,
    Blessings that we cannot name:
Whilst hosannas we are singing,
    May our hearts in rapture move;
Feel new grace in them still springing,
    Breathe the air of purest love.

2 Let us sail in grace's ocean,
    Float on that unbounded sea,
Guided into pure devotion,
    Kept from paths of error free:
On thy heav'nly manna feeding,
    Screen'd from ev'ry envious foe:
Love, O love for sinners bleeding,
    All for thee we would forego.

3 Keep us, Lord, still in communion
    Daily nearer drawn to thee;
Sinking in the sweetest union,
    Of that heart-felt mistery.
Keep us safe from each delusion,
    Well protected from all harms;
Free from sin, and all confusion,
    Circle us within thine arms.

HYMN XXXI.

1 CHRIST, from whom all bleſſings flow,
  Comforting thy ſaints below,
Hear us, who thy nature ſhare,
Who thy myſtic body are:
Join us in one ſpirit, join,
Let us ſtill receive of thine,
Still for more on thee we call,
Thee, who filleſt all in all.

2 Move, and actuate, and guide,
Diverſe gifts to each divide;
Plac'd according to thy will,
Let us all our work fulfil:
Never from our office move,
Needful to each other prove,
Uſe the grace on each beſtow'd,
Temper'd by the bleſſed God.

3 Many are we now, and one,
We, who Jeſus have put on;
There is neither bond nor free,
Male, nor female, Lord, in thee!
Love, like death, hath all deſtroy'd,
Render'd all diſtinctions void;
Names, and ſects, and parties fall,
Thou, O Chriſt, art all in all!

HYMN XXXII.

1 DEAR Lord, we crave thy presence,
    We thirst thy grace to prove;
We cannot bear thine absence,
    Nor live without thy love;
Come make us all one spirit,
    In thee, our common Lord,
And let thy blood and merit
    True gladness here afford.

2 Thy infinite compassion
    Once mov'd thee to come down;
To work out our salvation,
    Thou left'st thy father's throne:
Again repeat the favour,
    And make our spices flow;
And let us feel the favour
    Of thy perfumes below.

3 O sweetest, blessed Jesus,
    Now specify thy worth,
And let thy name be precious,
    As ointment poured forth:
Display thy bloody banner
    Before the eye of faith,
And get thyself the honour,
    Both in our life and death.

HYMN XXXIII.

1 FAR from our thoughts, vain world, be gone,
Let our religious hours alone;
O may our eyes the Saviour see,
We wait a visit, Lord, from thee.

2 O warm our hearts with holy fire,
And kindle there a pure desire;
Come, dearest Saviour from above,
And feed our souls with heav'nly love.

3 Bless'd Jesus, what delicious fare!
How sweet thy entertainments are!
Never did angels taste above,
Redeeming grace, and dying love.

4 Hail, great Immanuel, all divine;
In thee thy father's glories shine!
Thou brightest, sweetest, fairest one,
That eyes have seen, or angels known.

HYMN XXXIV.

1 O Let thy love our hearts constrain,
Jesus, the crucify'd!
What hast thou done our hearts to gain,
Languish'd, and groan'd, and dy'd!

2 Us into closest union draw,
    And in our inward parts
  Let kindness sweetly write her law,
    Let love command our hearts.

3 Who wou'd not now pursue the way,
    Where Jesus footsteps shine?
  Who would not own the pleasing sway
    Of charity divine?

4 O let us find the antient way,
    Our wond'ring foes to move,
  And force the heathen world to say,
    " See how these Christians love!"

HYMN XXXV.

1 JESUS, thou everlasting king,
    Accept the tribute which we bring,
  Accept thy well-deserv'd renown,
  And wear our praises as thy crown.

2 Let ev'ry act of worship be
  Like our espousals, Lord, to thee;
  Like the bless'd hour, when from above
  We first receiv'd thy pledge of love.

3 The

3 The gladness of that happy day,
  O may it ever, ever stay!
  Nor let our faith forsake its hold,
  Our hope decline, nor love grow cold!

4 Each foll'wing minute as it flies
  Increase thy praise, improve our joys,
  Till we are rais'd to sing thy name,
  At the great supper of the Lamb.

HYMN XXXVI.

AT DISMISSION.

1 Dismiss us with thy blessing, Lord,
    Help us to feed upon thy word:
  All that has been amiss forgive,
  And let thy truth within us live.

2 Tho' we are guilty, thou art good,
  Wash all our works in Jesu's blood;
  Give ev'ry fetter'd soul release,
  And bid us all depart in piece.

HYMN XXXVII.

MORNING.

1 RISE, my soul, adore thy maker
 Angels praise, join the lays,
  With them be partaker.

2 Sov'reign Lord of ev'ry spirit,
 In thy light lead me right,
  Thro' my Saviour's merit.

3 Thou this night wast my protector,
 With me stay, all this day,
  Ever my director.

4 Leave me not, but ever love me,
 Let thy peace be my bliss,
  Till thou hence remove me.

5 Holy, holy, holy giver
 Of all good, life and food,
  Reign ador'd for ever.

6 Glory, honour, thanks, and blessing,
 One in Three, give we thee,
  Never, never ceasing.

HYMN XXXVIII.

EVENING.

1 'ERE I sleep for ev'ry favour,
   This day shew'd by my God,
I will bless my Saviour.

2 O my Lord! what shall I render
   To thy name, still the same,
Gracious good and tender.

3 Leave me not, but ever love me,
   Let thy peace be my bliss,
Till thou hence remove me.

4 Visit me with thy salvation,
   Let thy care now be near,
Round my habitation.

5 Thou, my rock, my guard, my tow'r,
   Safely keep, while I sleep,
Me, with all thy pow'r.

6 And, whene'er in death I slumber,
   Let me rise with the wise,
Counted in their number.

HYMN XXXIX.

THE SAME.

1 NO farther go to-night, but stay,
Dear Saviour, till the break of day,
Turn in, dear Lord, with me;
And in the morning when I wake,
Me in thine arms, my Jesus, take,
And I'll go on with thee.

HYMN XL.

MORNING.

1 AWAKE, my soul, and with the sun,
Thy daily stage of duty run;
Shake off dull sloth, and early rise
To pay thy morning sacrifice.

2 Redeem thy mis-spent time that's past,
Live this day as if 'twere thy last;
T' improve thy talents take due care,
'Gainst the great day thyself prepare.

3 Let all thy converse be sincere,
Thy conscience as the noon-day clear;
Think how th' all-seeing God thy ways,
And all thy secret thought surveys.

4 Glory

4 Glory to God, who safe hath kept,
And hath refresh'd me while I slept;
Grant, Lord, when I from death shall wake,
I may of endless life partake.

5 Direct, controul, suggest this day,
All I design, or do, or say;
That all my pow'rs, with all their might,
In thy sole glory may unite.

6 Praise God, from whom all blessings flow,
Praise him all creatures here below;
Praise him above, ye heav'nly host,
Praise Father, Son, and Holy Ghost.

HYMN XLI.

EVENING.

1 GLORY to thee, my God, this night,
For all the blessings of the light;
Keep me, O keep me, king of kings,
Under thine own almighty wings.

2 Forgive me, Lord, for thy dear son,
Whatever ills this day I've done;
That with the world, myself, and thee,
I, 'ere I sleep, at peace may be.

3 Teach me to live that I may dread
The grave as little as my bed;
Teach me to die, that so I may
Triumphing rise at the last day.

4 O may my soul on thee repose,
And with sweet sleep my eye-lids close;
Sleep that may me more vig'rous make,
To serve my God when I awake.

5 Let my blest guardian, while I sleep,
Close to my bed his vigils keep;
Let no vain dream, disturb my rest,
No pow'rs of darkness me molest.

6 Praise God from whom all blessings flow,
Praise him all creatures here below;
Praise him above, ye heav'nly host,
Praise Father, Son, and Holy Ghost.

HYMN XLII.

LORD's DAY MORNING.

1 TO-DAY God bids the faithful rest,
To-day he show'rs his grace;
Seek ye my face, the Lord hath said,
Lord, we will seek thy face.

2 Come, let us leave the things of earth,
    With God's affembly join;
  Lo! heaven defcends to welcome man,
    To tafte the things divine!

3 We come, dear Saviour, lo! we come,
    Lord of our life and foul;
  We come difeas'd, and faint, and fick,
    Be pleas'd to make us whole.

4 We thirft, and fly to thee, O Lord,
    Thou fountain-head of good;
  Filthy we come, and all unclean,
    O cleanfe us in thy blood.

5 O may we pleafe our God to-day,
    May that be all our care!
  Give, Lord, thy grace, left evil thoughts
    Should mingle in our prayer.

6 Amidft th' affembly of thy faints
    Let us be faithful found;
  And let us join in humble pray'r,
    And in thy praife abound.

7 Let thy good fpirit help our fouls,
    With faith thy word to hear;
  Be with us in thy temple, Lord,
    And let us find thee near.

HYMN XLIII.

LORD's DAY EVENING.

1 WHEN, O dear Jesus, when shall I
    Behold thee all serene?
Blest in perpetual sabbath-day,
    Without a veil between?

2 Assist me while I wander here,
    Amidst a world of cares;
Incline my heart to pray with love,
    And then accept my pray'rs.

3 Release my soul from ev'ry chain,
    No more hell's captive led;
And pardon a repenting child,
    For whom the Saviour bled.

4 Spare me, my God, O spare the soul,
    That gives itself to thee;
Take all that I possess below,
    And give thyself to me.

5 Thy spirit, O my father, give,
    To be my guide and friend,
To light my way to ceaseless joys,
    Where sabbaths never end.

HYMN XLIV.

FOR NEW YEAR's DAY.

1 THE Lord of earth and sky,
    The God of ages praise!
  Who reigns enthron'd on high,
    Antient of endless days,
Who lengthens out our trial here,
And spares us yet another year.

2   Barren and wither'd trees,
    We cumber'd long the ground;
  No fruit of holiness
    On our dead souls was found;
Yet did he us in mercy spare,
Another, and another year.

3   When justice barr'd the sword,
    To cut the fig-tree down,
  The pity of our Lord
    Cry'd—" Let it still alone:"
The father mild inclin'd his ear,
And spar'd us yet another year.

4   Jesus, thy speaking blood
    From God obtain'd the grace,
  Who therefore hath bestow'd
    On us a longer space:
Thou didst in our behalf appear,
And lo! we see another year.

5 Then

5 Then dig about our root,
    Break up our fallow ground,
  And let our gracious fruit
    To thy great praise abound;
O let us all thy praise declare,
And fruit unto perfection bear.

HYMN XLV.

CIRCUMCISION.

1 SEE, my soul, with wonder see
    The incarnate deity;
Human nature he assumes,
He to ransom sinners comes:
He was not conceiv'd in sin,
He was infinitely clean;
Him no sinful spot disguis'd,
Yet lo! he was circumcis'd.

2 He fulfill'd all righteousness,
Standing in our legal place;
From the manger to the cross,
All he did he did for us:
He did all our woes retrieve,
He expir'd that we might live;
By his stripes our wounds are heal'd,
By his blood our peace is seal'd.

3 Jesu's

3 Jesu's pain procures our ease,
  Jesu's death is our release;
  Jesu's cross obtains our crown,
  Jesu's sepulchre our throne:
  Lord, conform us to thy death,
  Bid our sins yield up their breath;
  By thy resurrection's pow'r,
  Make our souls to glory soar.

4 Circumcise our filthy hearts,
  Purify our inward parts;
  Lord, destroy the carnal mind,
  That in thee we peace may find:
  In thy righteousness array'd,
  Let us triumph, and be glad;
  Let us walk with thee in white,
  Till we see thy face in light.

HYMN XLVI.

EPIPHANY.

1 SONS of men, behold from far,
    Hail the long-expected star;
  Jacob's star, that gilds the night,
  Guides bewilder'd nature right.

2 Fear not hence that there should flow
 Wars, or pestilence below;
 Wars it bids, and tumults cease,
 Ushering in the prince of peace.

3 Mild he shines on all beneath,
 Piercing **thro'** the shades of death;
 Scatt'ring error's wide-spread night,
 Kindling darkness into light.

4 Nations all far off and near,
 Haste to see your God appear;
 Haste, for him your hearts prepare,
 Meet him manifested there.

5 There behold the day-spring rise,
 Pouring eye-sight on your eyes;
 God in his own light survey,
 Shining to the perfect day.

6 **Sing,** ye morning stars, again,
 God descends on earth to reign!
 Deigns for man his life t' employ,
 Shout, ye sons of God, for joy.

HYMN XLVII.

GOOD-FRIDAY.

1 ALAS! and did my Saviour bleed?
  And did my sov'reign die?
Wou'd he devote that sacred head,
  For such a worm as I?

2 Was it for crimes that I had done,
  He groan'd upon the tree?
Amazing pity! grace unknown!
  And love beyond degree!

3 Well might the sun in darkness hide,
  And shut his glories in;
When God the mighty maker dy'd,
  For man the creature's sin.

4 Thus might I hide my blushing face,
  While his dear cross appears;
Dissolve my heart in thankfulness,
  And melt mine eyes to tears.

5 But drops of grief can ne'er repay
  The debt of love I owe;
Here, Lord, I give myself away,
  'Tis all that I can do.

HYMN XLVIII.

REPENTANCE AT THE CROSS.

1 OH! if my soul was form'd for woe,
    How could I vent my sighs!
  Repentance should like rivers flow
    From both my streaming eyes.

2 'Twas for my sins, my dearest Lord
    Hung on the cursed tree,
  And groan'd away a dying life,
    For thee, my soul, for thee.

3 O how I hate those lusts of mine,
    That crucify'd my God;
  Those sins that pierc'd and nail'd his flesh
    Fast to the fatal wood.

4 Yes, my redeemer, they shall die,
    My heart hath so decreed;
  Nor will I spare those guilty things
    That made my Saviour bleed.

5 Whilst with a melting broken heart,
    My murder'd Lord I view,
  I'll raise revenge against my sins,
    And slay the murd'rers too.

HYMN XLIX.

IT IS FINISHED.

1 " 'TIS finish'd," the Redeemer said,
    And meekly bow'd his dying head;
  Whilst we this sentence scan,
Come, sinners, and observe the **word**,
Behold the conquests of our Lord,
  Compleat for helpless man.

2 Finish'd the righteousness of grace,
Finish'd for sinner's pard'ning peace;
  Their mighty debt is paid:
Accusing law cancell'd by blood,
And **wrath of an** offended God
  In sweet oblivion laid.

3 Who now shall urge a second claim,
The law no longer can condemn,
  Faith a release can shew:
Justice itself a friend appears,
The prison-house a whisper hears,
  " Loose him, and let him go."

4 O unbelief, injurious bar!
  Source of tormenting, fruitless fear,
    Why dost thou yet reply?
Where'er thy loud objections fall,
" 'Tis finish'd," still may answer all
  And silence ev'ry cry.

5 His

5 His toil divinely finish'd stands,
  But ah! the praise his work demands,
    Careful may we attend!
  Conclusion to our souls be this,
  Because salvation finish'd is,
    Our thanks shall never end.

HYMN L.

CHRIST PIERCED.

1 IS there a thing beneath the sky,
    Can comfort bring, or satisfy,
      But our dear Saviour's wounds?
    Here is a sweet and constant peace,
    A treasure full of richest grace,
      All else are empty sounds.

2 Attend, my soul, sink down with shame,
  Before his face, who only came
    To suffer, bleed, and die:
  O think upon thy sin and guilt,
  For which his precious blood was spilt,
    Thou didst him crucify.

3 See thou vile piece of sinful dust,
  Thy dearest Lord sweat for thy lust,
    Till drops of blood fall down!
  See how he yonder prostrate lies!
  Observe his mournful pray'r and cries,
    Mark ev'ry tear and groan!

4 See

4 See thy dear Lord dragg'd like a thief,
  Amidst contempt, and stripes, and grief,
    For thee a sacrifice:
Fasten'd unto the shameful wood,
Despis'd by men, and bath'd in blood,
    So dear thy ransom price!

5 Lord dost thou suffer thus for me,
  Dost thou feel all this misery,
    To give me life and peace?
Then let me bear it on my heart,
My all is purchas'd with thy smart,
    Thy blood signs my release.

HYMN LI.

CHRIST CRUCIFIED.

1 O Love divine, what hast thou done!
    Th' immortal God hath dy'd for me,
  The father's co-eternal son
    Bore all my sins upon the tree;
  Th' immortal God for me hath dy'd,
  My Lord, my love is crucify'd!

2 Behold him all ye that pass by,
    The bleeding prince of life and peace;
  Come see, ye worms, your maker die,
    And say was ever love like his;
  Come feel with me his blood apply'd,
  My Lord, my love is crucify'd!

3 His

3 Is crucify'd for me and you,
    To bring us rebels back to God,
Believe, believe the record true,
    We are all bought with Jesu's blood;
Pardon and life flow from his side,
My Lord, my love is crucify'd!

4 Then let us sit beneath his cross,
    And gladly catch the healing stream;
All things for him account but loss,
    And give up all our hearts to him:
Of nothing speak, or think beside,
But Jesus and him crucify'd!

HYMN LII.

EASTER-DAY.

1 JESUS, who dy'd a world to save,
   Revives, and rises from the grave,
    By his almighty pow'r:
From sin, and death, and hell set free,
He captive leads captivity,
    And lives to die no more.

2 Children of God, look up and see,
   Your Saviour cloath'd with majesty,
    Triumphant o'er the tomb:
Give o'er your griefs, cast off your fears,
In heav'n your mansions he prepares,
    And soon will take you home.

3 His church is still his joy and crown,
   He looks with love and pity down,
     On her he did redeem:
   He tastes her joys, he feels her woes,
   And prays that she may spoil her foes,
     And ever reign with him.

4 O may we all from sin awake,
   May all in heav'n our places take,
     Near our exalted head!
   May all our souls to heav'n aspire,
   In thought, in will, in strong desire,
     To carnal pleasures dead!

HYMN LIII.

ANOTHER.

1 CHRIST the Lord is ris'n to-day,
   Sons of men and angels say!
   Raise your joys and triumphs high,
   Sing, ye heav'ns, and earth reply.

2 Love's redeeming work is done,
   Fought the fight, the battle won;
   Lo! our sun's eclipse is o'er,
   Lo! he sits in blood no more.

3 Vain the stone, the watch, the seal,
   Christ hath burst the gates of hell:
   Death in vain forbids his rise,
   Christ hath open'd paradise.

4 Lives again our glorious king,
   Where, O death, is now thy sting!
   Once he dy'd our souls to save,
   Where thy victory, O grave?

5 Soar we now where Christ hath led,
   Foll'wing our exalted head;
   Made like him, like him we rise,
   Ours the cross, the grave, the skies.

6 What tho' once we perish'd all,
   Partners of our parents fall;
   Second life we all receive,
   In our heav'nly Adam live.

7 Hail the Lord of earth and heav'n!
   Praise to thee by both be giv'n!
   Thee we greet triumphant now,
   Hail the resurrection — thou!

8 King of glory! soul of bliss!
   Everlasting life is this —
   Thee to know — thy pow'r to prove,
   Thus to sing, and thus to love.

HYMN

HYMN LIV.

ANOTHER.

1 THE sun of righteousness appears,
  To set in blood no more!
Adore the scatt'rer of your fears,
  Your rising sun adore.

2 The saints, when he resign'd his breath,
  Unclos'd their sleeping eyes;
He breaks again the bands of death,
  Again the dead arise.

3 Alone the dreadful race he ran,
  Alone the wine-press trod;
He dy'd, and suffer'd as a man,
  He rises as a God.

4 In vain the stone, the watch, the seal,
  Forbid an early rise,
To him who breaks the gates of hell,
  And opens paradise.

HYMN LV.

THE RESURRECTION AND ASCENSION OF CHRIST.

1 HOSANNA to the prince of light,
　　That cloath'd himself in clay;
　Enter'd the iron gates of death,
　　And tore the bars away.

2 Death is no more the king of dread,
　　Since our Immanuel rose;
　He took the tyrant's sting away,
　　And spoil'd her hellish foes.

3 See how the conqu'ror mounts aloft,
　　And to his father flies;
　With scars of honour in his flesh,
　　And triumph in his eyes.

4 Raise your devotion, mortal tongues,
　　To reach his blest abode;
　Sweet be the accents of our songs,
　　To our incarnate God.

5 Bright angels strike your loudest strings,
　　Your sweetest voices raise;
　Let heav'n, and all created things,
　　Sound our Immanuel's praise.

HYMN LVI.

ANOTHER.

1 YE that seek the Lord, who dy'd,
  Your God for sinners crucify'd;
Prevent the earliest dawn, and come
To worship at his sacred tomb:
Bring the sweet spices of your sighs,
Your contrite hearts, and streaming eyes,
Your sad complaints, and humble fears,
And embalm him with your tears.

2 While ye thus your souls employ,
Your sorrows shall be turn'd to joy;
Now, now let all your grief be o'er,
Believe, and ye shall weep no more:
An earthquake hath the cavern shook,
And burst the door, and rent the rock;
The Lord hath sent his angel down,
Who hath roll'd away the stone.

3 See, as snow his garment white,
His countenance as lightning bright;
He sits, and waves a flaming sword,
And waits upon his rising Lord:
The third auspicious morn is come,
And calls the Saviour from the tomb;
The bands of death are torn away,
And the tomb gives back its prey.

4 See, the Lord is ris'n indeed,
  To death deliver'd in your stead;
  His rise proclaims your sins forgiv'n,
  And shews the living way to heav'n:
  Go tell the foll'wers of your Lord,
  Their Jesus is to life restor'd;
  He lives, that they his life may find,
  Lives, to quicken all mankind.

HYMN LVII.

ASCENSION.

1 HAIL the day, that sees him rise,
     Ravish'd from our wishful eyes!
  Christ awhile to mortals giv'n,
  Re-ascends his native heav'n:
  There the pompous triumph waits,
  Lift your heads eternal gates!
  Wide unfold the radient scene,
  Take the king of glory in!

2 Him, tho' highest heav'n receives,
  Still he loves the earth he leaves;
  Tho' returning to his throne,
  Still he calls mankind his own:
  Still for us he intercedes,
  Prevalent his death he pleads;
  Next himself prepares our place,
  Harbinger of human race.

3 Master (may we ever say)
  Taken from our head to day;
  See thy faithful servants, see,
  Ever gazing up to thee!
  Grant, tho' parted from our sight,
  High above yon azure height:
  Grant our hearts may thither rise,
  Foll'wing thee beyond the skies.

4 Ever upward let us move,
  Wafted on the wings of love;
  Looking when our Lord shall come,
  Longing, gasping after home:
  There we shall with thee remain
  Partners of thine endless reign;
  There thy face unclouded see,
  Find our heav'n of heav'n in thee.

HYMN LVIII.

WHITSUNDAY.

1 JESU, we hang upon the word,
    Our longing souls have heard from thee;
  Be mindful of thy promise, Lord,
  Thy promise made to all, and me:
  Thy foll'wers, who thy steps pursue,
  And dare believe that God is true.

2 Thou saidst, I will the father pray,
And he the holy Ghost shall give,
Shall give him in your hearts to stay,
And never more his temples leave:
Myself will to my children come,
And make them mine eternal home.

3 Come then, dear Lord, thyself reveal,
And let thy promise now take place;
Be it according to thy will,
According to thy word of grace:
Thy sorrowful disciples chear,
And send us down the comforter.

4 He visits now the troubled breast,
And oft relieves our sad complaint;
But soon we lose the transient guest,
But soon we drop again, and faint:
Repeat the melancholy moan —
"Our joy is fled, our comfort gone."

5 Send him, O Lord, into each heart,
Our sure, inseparable guide:
O might we meet, and never part;
O might he in our hearts abide,
And keep his house of praise and pray'r,
And rest, and reign for ever there.

HYMN

HYMN LIX.

TO THE TRINITY.

1 PRAISE be to the Father giv'n,
  Christ he gave,
  Us to save,
 Now the heirs of heav'n.

2 Pay we equal adoration
  To the son,
  He alone
 Wrought out our salvation.

3 Glory to th' eternal spirit,
  Us he seals,
  Christ reveals,
 And applies his merit.

4 Worship, honour, thanks, and blessing,
  One in three,
  Give we thee,
 Never, never ceasing.

HYMN LX.

THE NATIVITY.

1 HArk the glad found! the Saviour comes,
　　The Saviour promis'd long!
　Let every heart prepare a throne,
　　And every voice a fong.

2 On him the Spirit largely pour'd,
　　Exerts its facred fire;
　Wifdom and might, and zeal, and love,
　　His holy breaft infpire.

3 He comes the pris'ners to releafe,
　　In Satan's bondage held;
　The gates of brafs before him burft,
　　The iron fetters yield.

4 He comes, from thickeft films of vice
　　To clear the mental ray;
　And on the eye-balls of the blind,
　　To pour celeftial day.

5 He comes the broken heart to bind,
　　The bleeding foul to cure;
　And with the riches of his grace,
　　T'enrich the humble poor.

6 Our glad hosannas, prince of peace,
   Thy welcome shall proclaim;
  And heav'n's eternal arches ring
   With thy beloved name.

HYMN LXI.

ANOTHER.

1 HARK! the herald angels sing,
   Glory to the new-born king;
  Peace on earth, and mercy mild,
  God and sinners reconcil'd.
  Joyful all ye nations rise,
  Join the triumphs of the skies,
  With th' angelic host proclaim,
  " Christ is born in Bethlehem."

2 Christ, by highest heav'n ador'd,
  Christ the everlasting Lord;
  Late in time behold him come,
  Offspring of a virgin's womb:
  Veil'd in flesh, the Godhead see,
  Hail th' incarnate deity!
  Pleas'd as man, with men t'appear,
  Jesus, our Immanuel here.

3 Hail the heav'n-born prince of peace,
 Hail the sun of righteousness!
 Light and life to all he brings,
 Ris'n with healing in his wings:
 Mild he lays his glory by,
 Born, that man no more may die,
 Born to raise the sons of earth,
 Born to give the second birth.

4 Come, desire of nations, come,
 Fix in us thy humble home;
 Rise, the woman's conq'ring seed,
 Bruise in us the serpent's head:
 Adam's likeness now efface,
 Stamp thine image in its place;
 Second Adam from above,
 Re-instate us in thy love.

HYMN LXII.

THE SAME.

1 WHAT good news the angels bring!
   What glad tiding of our king!
 Christ the Lord is born to day,
 Christ who takes our sins away:
 He who rules in heav'n and earth,
 Hath in Bethlehem his birth;
 Him shall all his people see,
 And rejoice eternally.

2 Lift your hearts and voices high,
  With hosannas fill the sky;
  Glory be to God above,
  God is infinite in love:
  Peace on earth, good-will to men!
  Now with us our God is seen:
  Angels join with us in praise!
  Help to sing redeeming grace.

3 Now the wall is broken down,
  Now the gospel is made known;
  Now the door is open wide,
  Christ for jew and gentile dy'd.
  All who feel the weight of sin,
  All who languish to be clean;
  All who for redemption groan,
  May be sav'd by faith alone.

4 Jesus is the lovely name,
  This the angel doth proclaim;
  He shall all his people save,
  They in him remission have:
  When they see themselves undone,
  They take refuge in the son;
  They shall all be born again,
  And with him in glory reign.

5 Shout, ye nations of the earth,
   Sing the triumphs of his birth;
   All the world by him is bleſt,
   Sound his praiſe from eaſt to weſt:
   Jews and gentiles jointly ſing,
   Chriſt our common Lord and king;
   Chriſt our life, our joy, our ſong,
   To eternity prolong.

HYMN LXIII.

THE SAME.

1 COME, thou long expected Jeſus!
      Born to ſet thy people free;
   From our fears and ſins releaſe us,
      Let us find our reſt in thee!
   Iſrael's ſtrength and conſolation,
      Hope of all the earth thou art;
   Dear deſire of ev'ry nation,
      Joy of ev'ry longing heart!

2 Born thy people to deliver,
      Born a child, and yet a king;
   Born to reign in us for ever,
      Now thy gracious kingdom bring!
   By thine own eternal ſpirit,
      Rule in all our hearts alone;
   By thine all-ſufficient merit,
      Raiſe us to thy glorious throne.

HYMN LXIV.

SICKNESS, OR DIVINE CORRECTION.

1 HOW happy the sorrowful man,
    Whose sorrow is sent from above!
Indulg'd with a visit of pain,
    Chastiz'd by omnipotent love:
The author of all his distress
    He comes by affliction to know;
And God he in heaven shall bless,
    That ever he suffer'd below.

2 Thus, thus may I happily grieve,
    And hear the intent of his rod,
The marks of adoption receive,
    The strokes of a merciful God;
With nearer access to his throne,
    My burthen of folly confess,
The cause of my miseries own,
    And cry for an answer of peace.

3 O father of mercies on me,
    On me in affliction bestow
A pow'r of ayplying to thee,
    And sanctify'd use of my woe:
I would in a spirit of prayer,
    To all thy appointments submit;
The pledge of my happiness bear,
    And joyfully die at thy feet.

4 Then,

4 Then, father, and never till then,
   I all the felicity prove,
Of living a moment in pain,
   Of dying in Jesus's love:
A suff'rer here with my Lord,
   With Jesus above I sit down,
Receive an eternal reward,
   And glory obtain in a crown.

HYMN LXV.

A FUNERAL HYMN.

1 AH! lovely appearance of death,
   No sight upon earth is so fair;
Not all the gay pageants that breathe,
   Can with a dead body compare;
With solemn delight I survey
   The corpse when the spirit is fled,
In love with the beautiful clay,
   And longing to lie in its stead.

2 How blest is our brother, bereft
   Of all that could burthen his mind;
How easy the soul that hath left
   The wearisome body behind!
Of evil incapable thou,
   Whose relics with envy I see;
No longer in misery now,
   No longer a sinner like me.

3 This earth is affected no more
    With sickness, or shaken with pain;
The war in the members is o'er,
    And never shall vex him again:
No anger henceforward, or shame,
    Shall redden this innocent clay,
Extinct is the animal flame,
    And passion is vanish'd away.

4 This languishing head is at rest,
    Its thinking and aching are o'er;
This quiet immoveable breast
    Is heav'd by affliction no more;
This heart is no longer the seat
    Of trouble and torturing pain;
It ceases to flutter and beat,
    It never shall flutter again.

5 The lids he so seldom could close,
    By sorrow forbidden to sleep,
Seal'd up in eternal repose,
    Have strangely forgotten to weep:
The fountains could yield no supplies,
    These hollows from water are free;
The tears are all wip'd from these eyes,
    And evil they never shall see.

6 To mourn and to suffer is mine,
    While bound in a prison I breathe;
And still for deliverance pine,
    And press to the issues of death:

What now with my tears I bedew,
  O might I this moment become;
My spirit created anew,
  My flesh be consign'd to the tomb!

HYMN LXVI.

ANOTHER.

1 HOsanna to Jesus on high!
    Another has enter'd his rest;
  Another is 'scap'd to the sky,
    And lodg'd in Immanuel's breast:
  The soul of our brother is gone
    To heighten the triumph above;
  Exalted to Jesus's throne!
  Exalted by Jesus's love!

2 How happy the angels that fall
    Transported at Jesus's name!
  The saints, whom he soonest shall call
    To share in the feast of the Lamb!
  No longer imprison'd in clay,
    Who next from this dungeon shall fly?
  Who first shall be summon'd away?
    My merciful God — Is it I?

3 O Jesus, if this be thy will,
    That suddenly I should depart,
  Thy council of mercy reveal,
    And whisper the call to my heart:

O give me a signal to know
    If soon thou wouldst have me remove,
And leave the dull body below,
    And fly to the regions of love.

HYMN LXVII.

ANOTHER.

1 AND let this feeble body fail,
    And let it faint or die!
My soul shall quit the mournful vale,
    And soar to worlds on high:
Shall join the disembody'd saints,
    And find its long-sought rest,
That only bliss for which it pants,
    In the Redeemer's breast.

2 In hope of that immortal crown,
    I now the cross sustain,
And gladly wander up and down,
    And smile at toil and pain:
I suffer on my threescore years,
    Till my deliv'rer comes,
And wipes away his servant's tears,
    And takes his exile home.

3 O what hath Jesus bought for me,
    Before my ravish'd eyes!
Rivers of life divine I see,
    And trees of paradise:

I see a world of spirits bright,
    Who taste the pleasure's there;
They all are rob'd in spotless white,
    And conq'ring palms they bear.

4 O what are all my suff'rings here,
    If, Lord, thou count me meet,
With that enraptur'd host t' appear,
    And worship at thy feet!
Give joy or grief, give ease or pain,
    Take life and friends away!
But let me find them all again,
    In that eternal day!

HYMN LXVIII.

LIFE AND ETERNITY.

1 THEE we adore, eternal name,
    And humbly own to thee
How feeble is our mortal frame,
    What dying worms we be!

2 Our wasting lives grow shorter still,
    As months and days increase,
And every beating pulse we tell
    Leaves one the number less.

3 The year rolls round, and steals away
   The breath that first it gave;
Whate'er we do, where'er we be,
   We're trav'ling to the grave.

4 Dangers stand thick thro' all the ground
   To push us to the tomb;
And fierce diseases wait around,
   To hurry mortals home.

5 Great God! on what a slender thread
   Hang everlasting things;
Th' eternal states of all the dead,
   Upon life's feeble strings.

6 Infinite joy, or endless woe
   Attend on every breath;
And yet how unconcern'd we go
   Upon the brink of death!

7 Waken, O Lord, our drowsy sense,
   To walk this dang'rous road;
And if our souls are hurried hence,
   May they be found with God.

HYMN LXIX.

DEATH AND GLORY.

1 MY soul, come meditate the day,
    And think how near it stands,
When thou must quit this house of clay,
    And fly to unknown lands.

2 And you, mine eyes, look down and view
    The hollow gaping tomb;
This gloomy prison waits for you,
    Whene'er the summons come.

3 Oh! could we die with those that die,
    And place us in their stead;
Then would our spirits learn to fly,
    And converse with the dead.

4 Then shou'd we see the saints above,
    In their own glorious forms,
And wonder why our souls shou'd love,
    To dwell with mortal worms.

5 How should we scorn these cloaths of flesh,
    These fetters, and this load;
And long for evening t' undress,
    That we may rest with God.

6 We shou'd almost forsake our clay,
    Before the summons come,
And pray, and wish our souls away
    To their eternal home.

HYMN LXX.

ANOTHER.

1 IN a world of sin and sorrow,
    Compass'd round with many a care,
From eternity we borrow
    Hope, that can exclude despair:
Thee triumphant God and Saviour!
    In the glass of faith we see;
O assist each faint endeavour!
    Raise our earth-born souls to thee.

2 Place that awful scene before us,
    Of the last tremendous day;
When to life thou shalt restore us,
    Ling'ring ages haste away!
Then this vile and sinful nature
    Incorruption shall put on;
Life renewing, glorious Saviour!
    Let thy gracious will be done.

HYMN LXXI.

ON THE DEATH OF A BELIEVER.

1 'TIS finish'd, 'tis done !
    The spirit is fled,
The pris'ner is gone,
    The christian is dead :
The christian is living
    Thro' Jesus his love,
And gladly receiving
    A kingdom above.

2 All honour and praise
    Is Jesus's due;
Supported by grace,
    He fought his way thro':
Triumphantly glorious,
    Thro' Jesus's zeal,
And more than victorious
    O'er sin, death, and hell.

3 Then let us record
    The conquering name,
Our captain and Lord,
    With shoutings proclaim:
Who trust in his passion,
    And follow our head,
To certain salvation
    We all shall be led.

4 O Jesus, lead on
　　Thy militant care,
And give us the crown
　　Of righteousness there:
Where dazzled with joy,
　　The seraphim gaze,
Or prostrate adore thee
　　In silence of praise.

5 Come, Lord, and display
　　Thy sign in the sky,
And bear us away
　　To mansions on high:
The kingdom be giv'n,
　　The purchase divine,
And crown us in heav'n
　　Eternally thine.

HYMN LXXII.

THE SECOND COMING OF CHRIST.

1 HE comes! he comes! the Saviour dear,
　　The seventh trumpet speaks him near;
His lightnings flash, his thunders roll,
He's welcome to the faithful soul,
　　Welcome, welcome, welcome, welcome,
　　welcome to the faithful soul.

2 From heav'n angelic voices found,
See th' almighty Jesus crown'd!
Girt with omnipotence and grace,
And glory decks the Saviour's face,
 Glory, glory, glory, glory, glory decks
 the Saviour's face.

3 Descending on his azure throne,
He claims the kingdoms as his own;
The kingdoms all obey his word,
And hail him their triumphant Lord,
 Hail him, hail him, hail him, hail him,
 hail him their triumphant Lord.

4 Shout, all the people of the sky,
And all the saints of the most high:
Our God, who now his right obtains,
For ever, and for ever reigns,
 Ever, ever, ever, ever, ever, and for
 ever reigns.

5 The father praise, the son adore,
The spirit bless for evermore:
Salvation's glorious work is done,
We welcome the great three in one,
 Welcome, welcome, welcome, welcome,
 welcome the great three in one.

HYMN LXXIII.

JUDGMENT.

1. LO! he cometh, countless trumpets
    Blow before the bloody sign;
  'Midst ten thousand saints and angels,
    See the crucified shine.
        Hallelujah! hallelujah! hallelujah!
  Welcome, welcome, bleeding Lamb!

2 Now his merit, by the harpers,
    Thro' th' eternal deep resounds;
  Now resplendent shine his nail-prints,
    Ev'ry eye shall see his wounds:
        They who pierc'd him, they who
            pierc'd him, they who pierc'd him,
  Shall at his appearance wail.

3 Ev'ry island, sea, and mountain,
    Heav'n and earth shall flee away;
  All who hate him, must, ashamed,
    Hear the trump proclaim the day:
        Come to judgment, come to judg-
            ment, come to judgment,
  Stand before the son of man.

4 Saints

4 Saints who love him, view his glory
   Shining in his bruised face,
His dear person on the rainbow,
   Now his peoples head shall raise:
      Happy mourners, happy mourners,
        happy mourners,
   Lo! in clouds he comes, he comes!

5 Now redemption, long expected,
   See in solemn pomp appear;
All his people once rejected,
   Now shall meet him in the air:
      Hallelujah! hallelujah! hallelujah!
   Now the promis'd kingdom's come.

6 View him smiling, now determin'd
   Ev'ry evil to destroy;
All the nations now shall sing him
   Songs of everlasting joy:
      O come quickly, O come quickly,
        O come quickly,
   Hallelujah! come, Lord, come.

GLORIA

GLORIA PATRI.

I.

TO Father, Son, and Holy Ghost,
    Thanks, praise, and glory be,
As was, and is, and shall be still,
    To all eternity.

II.

To God in persons three,
    All glory be therefore,
As in beginning was, is now,
    And shall be evermore.

III.

To Father, Son, and Holy Ghost,
Be praise amidst the heav'nly host,
    And in the church below;
From whom all creatures drew their breath,
By whom redemption bless'd the earth,
    From whom all comforts flow.

IV.

Praise God, from whom all blessings flow,
Praise him all creatures here below;
Praise him above, ye heav'nly host,
Praise Father, Son, and Holy Ghost.

V.

Sing we to our God above,
Praise eternal as his love:
Praise him, all ye heav'nly host,
Father, Son, and Holy Ghost.

AN INDEX

TO THE

PSALMS AND HYMNS.

A

	Page
AUTHOR of true and saving faith	31
Ah, Lord, how faithless is my heart	103
Arise, my soul, my joyful pow'rs	118
All ye that pass by	120
Array'd in mortal flesh	138
Arise, my tend'rest thoughts, arise	145
A charge to keep I have	146
Awake, and sing the song	148
A thousand foes prepare to war	163

B

Be with me, Lord, where'er I go	82
Blessed are the sons of God	95
Brethren let us join to bless	165
Blest are the souls that hear and know	168
Bless, O my soul, the living God.	181

C Come

C

	Page
Come, ye sinners, poor and wretched	3
Come, sinners, to the gospel-feast	7
Come, ye sinners, come to Jesus	13
Come, thou almighty king	16
Come, O thou universal good	49
Come let us join our chearful songs	64
Come let us all unite to praise	79
Children of Israel, see what shade	94
Come, ye that love the Lord	135
Come, thou fount of ev'ry blessing	149
Children of the heav'nly king	153

D

Dear Lord, attend my pray'r	40
Dearest Jesus, come to me	89
Disciples of Christ	98
Descend from heav'n, immortal dove	182

F

Father, I stretch my hands to thee	24
Father, (if thou my Father art)	102
From thee, my God, my joys shall rise	114
Father, how wide thy glory shines	172

G

Glory to God, who gave the word	20
Great God! indulge my humble claim	34

God

INDEX.

	Page
God of my salvation, hear	35
Ground, O ground me on the Lamb	38
Give to our God immortal praise	104
Glory be to God on high, hallelujah!	141
God of all consolation, take	167
God of all grace and majesty	174

H

How sad our state by nature is	26
How, my dear Lord, shall I express	59
How heavy is the night	65
Happy the heart where graces reign	67
How blest are they, whose feet have found	75
Hail, thou once despised Jesus	78
How can we adore	84
Hail, alpha and omega, hail	92
How oft have sin and satan strove	129
He is a God of sov'reign love	144
Holy Lamb, who thee receive	176
How glorious the Lamb	183

I J

Jesu, Redeemer, Saviour, Lord	29
Jesu, friend of sinners, hear	36
Jesu, Jesu, king of saints	37
Jesus, vouchsafe to hear the cry	39
Jesus, I love thy charming name	63
Jesus, the Saviour of my soul	71
Jesu, lover of my soul	86

B b   Jesu

INDEX.

	Page
Jesu, thy blood and righteousness	88
Jesus my all, to heav'n is gone	122
Join all the glorious names	136
I long to behold him array'd	155
Jesus, thou art my righteousness	175

K

Kind is the speech of Christ our Lord	177

L

Let ev'ry mortal ear attend	6
Lord, we come before thee now	14
Long have we sat beneath the sound	19
Light of those whose dreary dwelling	25
Lord, if thou the grace impart	42
Lord, I am vile, conceiv'd in sin	53
Lord, I would spread my sore distress	56
Lo! to the hills I lift mine eyes	74
Let us, the sheep by Jesus nam'd	93
Lord and God of heav'nly pow'rs, hallelujah!	123
Love divine, all love excelling	131
Lord avenge thy tempted saints	139
Let me but hear my Saviour say	171
Lord Jesu, when, when shall it be	175
Lord, all I am is known to thee	180

M

Most righteous God, my doom I bear	30
My God, the spring of all my joys	68

INDEX.

	Page
My Saviour, my almighty friend	100
My dear Redeemer, dying Lord	111
My God, my life, my love	115
My God, my portion, and my love	119
My Lord, I'm fill'd with wonder	125
My Lord, how great's the favour	126
Meet and right it is to sing	134
My hiding-place, my refuge, tow'r	173

N

Now may the spirit's holy fire	11
Now begin the heav'nly theme	80
Not all the blood of beasts	147

O

Once more we come before our God	12
O God of wisdom, God of might	18
O sun of righteousness, arise	22
O Lord, to whom for help I call	28
O for an heart to love my God	33
On thee, O God of purity	43
O that the Lord would guide my way	44
Oft hast thou, Lord, in tender love	45
O my Lord, what must I do	48
O that my load of sin was gone	50
O what shall I do my Saviour to praise	51
O thou that hear'st when sinners cry	54
O dearest Lord, give me an heart	62
Of him who did salvation bring	76
O thou, in whom the Gentiles trust	77

INDEX.

	Page
O heavenly king	90
O come, thou wounded Lamb of God	96
O Jesu, Jesu, dearest Lord	97
O love, thou bottomless abyss	101
O thou tender loving Jesu	107
O for a thousand tongues to sing	109
O dear Redeemer, who alone	112
O Jesus, everlasting God	124
O love divine, how sweet thou art	130
Oft I reflect upon the grace	143
O what shall I do to retrieve	151
O Jesu, our Lord	156
O come let us join	169
O thou holy Lamb divine	170
O Lord my God, whose sov'reign love	179

P

Plung'd in a gulph of dark despair	117

R

Rejoice, the Lord is king	70
Rejoice evermore	73
Rise, my soul, and stretch thy wings	152

S

Sinners, obey the gospel-word	5
Sinners, behold the pierced Lamb	8
Son of God, thy blessing grant	27
Shew pity, Lord, O Lord, forgive	53

Sweet

INDEX.

	Page
Sweet was the hour, the minutes sweet	60
Salvation, O the joyful sound	91
Saviour, I do feel thy merit	105
Sweet is the mem'ry of thy grace	132
Stay, thou insulted spirit, stay	166

T

Thou hidden love of God, whose height	23
The one thing needful, that good part	46
The voice of my beloved sounds	52
That God of glorious majesty	57
The Saviour's love once truly known	69
Thou dear Redeemer, dying Lamb	87
Throughout the Saviour's life we trace	106
The glories of my maker, God	113
The despised Nazerene	128
Thou shepherd of Israel, and mine	150
This God is the God we adore	163
To God the only wife	178

W

We magnify thy grace, O Lord	15
With heart and lips unfeign'd	21
When, gracious Lord, when shall it be	47
With joy we meditate the grace	66
With all my pow'r of heart and tongue	110
When with my mind devoutly prest	141
What diff'rent pow'rs of grace and sin	154

INDEX.

	Page
When I survey the wond'rous cross	157
World adieu! thou real cheat	158
When all thy mercies, O my God	160
What shall we render unto thee	161
Why should I doubt his love at last	180

Y

Ye weary wanderers draw near	9
Ye servants of God	83

GLORIA PATRI, 275 & 276.

INDEX

TO THE

PSALMS

SELECTED FROM THE OLD VERSION.

	Page
A	
ALL laud and praife with heart and voice	194
All people that on earth do dwell	200
D	
Direct me in thy truth	193
H	
How perfect is the law of God	190
I	
Incline thine ears, O Lord, and let	187
I will give laud and honour both	196
I waited long, and fought the Lord	197
It is a thing both good and meet	198

M My

INDEX.

M
	Page
My shepherd is the living Lord	191
My soul give laud unto the Lord	201

O
O Lord our God, how wonderful	188
O Holy Ghost, into our souls	202
O Lord, turn not thy face away	203

S
Sing ye with praise unto the Lord	199

T
The man is blest, that hath not lent	185

W
Within thy tabernacle, Lord	189
Who is the man, O Lord, that shall	192

Y
Ye righteous in the Lord, rejoice	195

INDEX

TO THE

SACRAMENT AND FESTIVAL HYMNS.

A
	Page
ARISE, my foul, with wonder fee	214
All praife to the Lord	216
All glory and praife	221
Awake, my foul, and with the fun	242
Alas! and did my Saviour bleed	251
Ah! lovely appearance of death	272
And let this feeble body fail	275

C
Come, deareft Lord, defcend and dwell	208
Come, O my foul, and fing	227
Come, holy fpirit, heav'nly dove	229
Come, defcend, O heav'nly fpirit	234
Chrift, from whom all bleffings flow	255
Chrift the Lord is ris'n to-day	257
Come, thou long expected Jefus	270

D
Dear Lord, we crave thy prefence	236
Difmifs us with thy bleffing, Lord	239

E 'Ere

INDEX.

E
	Page
'Ere I sleep, for ev'ry favour	241

F
Father, God, who see'ft in me	209
Father of mankind	223
Far from our thoughts, vain world, be gone	237

G
God of all redeeming grace	215
Glory to thee, my God this night	243

H
Hosanna to the prince of light	260
Hail the day, that sees him rise	262
Hark the glad sound! the Saviour comes	266
Hark, the herald angels sing	267
How happy the sorrowful man	271
Hosanna to Jesus on high	274
He comes! he comes! the Saviour dear	281

I J
Jesu, dear redeeming Lord	212
Jesus invites his saints	219
Jesu, suffering deity	226
Jesu, Lord, we look to thee	231
Jesu, we thy promise claim	233
Jesus, thou everlasting king	238
Is there a thing beneath the sky	254

Jesus,

INDEX.

	Page
Jesus, who dy'd a world to save	256
Jesu, we hang upon the word	263
In a world of sin and sorrow	279

L
Lamb of God, for whom we languish	210
Lord, how divine thy comforts are	211
Lamb of God, whose bleeding love	224
Lo! he cometh, countless trumpets	283

M
My soul, come meditate the day	278

N
No farther go to night, but stay	242

O
Our shepherd alone	217
O Jesus, my love	219
Our lives, our blood we here present	226
O let thy love our hearts constrain	237
Oh! if my soul was form'd for woe	252
O love divine, what hast thou done	255

P
Praise be to the Father giv'n	265

R
Rise, my soul, adore thy maker	240

INDEX.

S

	Page
Sitting around our father's board	227
Still, O Lord, our faith increase	232
See, my soul, with wonder see	248
Sons of men, behold from afar	249

T

This day the Lord of hosts invites	208
The Lord, how glorious is his face	213
Together with these symbols, Lord	215
Thou very paschal Lamb	218
Thankful for our ev'ry blessing	222
Try us, O God, and search the ground	230
To-day God bids the faithful rest	244
The Lord of earth and sky	247
" 'Tis finish'd," the Redeemer said	253
The sun of righteousness appears	259
Thee we adore, eternal name	276
" 'Tis finish'd," 'tis done	80

W

We sing th' amazing deeds	225
When, O dear Jesus, when shall I	246
What good news the angels bring	268

Y

Ye that seek the Lord who dy'd	261

F I N I S.

www.ingramcontent.com/pod-product-compliance
Lightning Source LLC
Chambersburg PA
CBHW030818230426
43667CB00008B/1280